Art Outhouse
Bathroom Book

a Newfoundland & Labrador book of lists

Harry Cuff Publications Limited
St. John's : 1996

© 1996 Copyright Art Rockwood

All rights reserved. No part of this book may be reproduced or transmitted in any form or by any means without the written permission of the author and the publisher.

Publisher's Acknowledgements

Appreciation is expressed to the Canada Council for publication assistance.

CIP available upon request

ISBN 1-896338-06-2

Printed by
Robinson-Blackmore Printing and Publishing Ltd., St. John's

Published by
Harry Cuff Publications Limited
94 LeMarchant Road
St. John's, Newfoundland
A1C 2H2

Contents

INTRODUCTION 7
CULTURE AND HERITAGE 8

Ten early descriptions of Newfoundland and Labrador 11
Seven snappy comebacks 12
Weather sayings 13
Ice conditions 13
Ten Beothuk words 14
Three uses for a haddock 14
Heritage buildings 14
Threatened heritage structures 15
Lost treasures of Newfoundland architecture 16
Newfoundland "survivals" 17
Two things you probably thought were Newfoundlandia but aren't 18
Favourite tipples 18
Newfoundland's ten rarest coins 19

POLITICS AND GOVERNMENT 20

The Prime Ministers of Newfoundland 20
Premiers of Newfoundland 21
Early Governors of Newfoundland 21
French Governors at Plaisance 21
Naval Governors of Newfoundland 22
Resident Governors of Newfoundland
(appointed after Newfoundland received colonial status) 23
Newfoundland communities re-named after colonial governors 24
Lieutenant-Governors of Newfoundland and Labrador 24
Twenty politicians, first elected to office under the age of 30 25
Ten resounding election victories 25
Ten political characters 27
Eight politicians in the wrong profession 29
Ten women who ran for public office 30
Longest service on municipal council 31
Longest service in federal or provincial politics 32
Districts which supported confederation by more than 3-1
in the second referendum of 1948 32

iii

Districts which supported Responsible Government in the
1948 referendum   33
Hardest-fought election campaigns   33

MARINE   35

Longest serving coastal steamers   35
The Alphabet Fleet   35
The Splinter Fleet   35
Bowring's Shakespeare Fleet   35
Ten books written by fishermen   36
Ten dramatic marine rescues   36
Graveyards of the Atlantic   39

ARTS AND LETTERS   39

Milestones in Newfoundland theatrical history   39
Fifteen Significant Newfoundland Plays   41
Denyse Lynde's list of influential actors/facilitators   42
Six major-release movies made in Newfoundland
(and one that may have been)   43
Great minds think alike: early Newfoundland trivia books   43
James Murphy's pursuits   45
James Murphy's "What Tourists Should Know of Newfoundland"
(May 1926)   46
Murphy's list of Newfoundlanders who held and
who hold high positions in other lands   46
Smallwood's Lists   48
Joey's prerequisites for the job of Premier of Newfoundland
and Labrador   48
Smallwood's own assessment of his personal qualifications
for the job of Premier   48
Smallwood's two indispensable qualifications for future
premiers of Newfoundland   49
Five admitted failures   49
J.R. Smallwood's list of the most interesting Newfoundlanders
of the 20th Century   49
J.R. Smallwood's list of great Newfoundland books   50
Bob Cuff's essential Newfoundlandia   51

PEOPLE   52

Nine American show business personalities who served in
Newfoundland with the U.S. forces   52
Ten American show business personalities who appeared in
Newfoundland during World War II   53
10 great seafaring families   53

Come From Aways—"Mainland" division	53
Come From Aways—American division	54
Come From Aways—International division	55
Ten Newfoundlanders who overcame their handicaps	56
Most common family names of the Island of Newfoundland (compiled by E.R. Seary)	56
Most common family names of Labrador (compiled from the 1995 telephone directory and voter's lists)	56
Beothuk indians who lived for a time in white society	56
Women in the Newfoundland public service in 1852	57
Influential Newfoundland and Labrador women	57

PLACES 58

Familiar coves	58
The most common names for an island	59
The most common names for a pond	59
Other points of interest	59
Most unusual placenames (abandoned communities)	60
Unusual placenames (current communities)	60
Most unusual placenames (Labrador division)	60
Placenames from Languages other than English or French	61
Small towns	61
Off the beaten track: unheralded Newfoundland beauty spots	62

OUR JUDICIARY AND LAWS 63

Sir Humphrey Gilbert's three laws	63
John Guy's Laws	63
Celebrated legal cases	64
Ten celebrated jurists	68

NOTABLE PEOPLE AND EVENTS 69

Six famous Newfoundland natives	69
Shanawdithit's gifts to William E. Cormack	69
Cormack's gifts to the Royal Scottish Museum in Edinburgh	69
Events which happened in Newfoundland that had a significant impact on the world	70
Ten Newfoundland contributions to polar exploration	71
Events elsewhere which had a great effect on Newfoundland	73
Early censuses	76
The official census	76
Family names recorded before 1670	77

MILITARY 78

Twenty significant events in Newfoundland military history	78
Eight Newfoundland battles	80
Five foreign battlefield parks which honour Newfoundlanders who fought in World War I	81

DISASTERS 81

The 13 most tragic marine disasters in Newfoundland waters	81
Three notable aviation disasters	83
Two tsunami	83
Famous fires	83

NATURAL HISTORY 85

Rare bird sightings	85
Hypothetical bird list for Newfoundland	86
Peter Scott's ten facts about Newfoundland and Labrador plants	86
Jim Butler's interesting geological formations	87
Extra-terrestrial objects	90
Fossil finds	91
Abandoned mines worth a visit	91

BUSINESS AND ENGINEERING 93

The oldest businesses in Newfoundland	93
Some more businesses that are at least 100 years old	93
Ten man-made marvels	94

RELIGION 94

Hans Rollmann's ten significant events in Newfoundland and Labrador religious history	94

SPORTS 95

Ten great Newfoundland and Labrador sports teams	96
Ten great moments in Newfoundland and Labrador sports history	98
Ten significant female athletes form Newfoundland and Labrador	102
Ten significant male athletes from Newfoundland and Labrador	104

ART ROCKWOOD'S LISTS OF "STUFF" 107

The "Rockwood Files" list of little-known historical landmarks and facts	107
Three great moments in Newfoundland radio and television history	109
Great Newfoundland web sites	110
Two of my most embarrassing moments	112
A chuckle to end with...	113
Famous last words	114

Introduction

Some time ago someone told me how much they enjoyed my previous Trivia books. I was flattered for a moment, until he said, "Yep... keep 'em on the flushbox all the time."

Now I have never had any pretence that my efforts to collect in print some favourite facts and yarns made me another Tolstoy. I have never laboured under the illusion that what I was writing was great literature. I have truly never wanted it to be. After all, there are a lot of copies of *War and Peace* that end up high on some oak bookshelf, never to have the binding cracked. And if "my" bookshelf was made of porcelain, at least the Trivia books were reaching their audience.

Maybe a bathroom book is not such a terrible thing for a Trivia book to be. Certainly, a lot of trivia books fit in that category. Perhaps there is something about the tranquillity of #19 that makes the trivial seem important. And trivia books tend to be written in short snippets, so perhaps that is how they should be read. So perhaps I'll go back to being flattered.

Art Rockwood's Newfoundland and Labrador Trivia and its sequel were largely anecdotal. This time I decided to offer something a little different. Lists, lists and more lists. But, the answer to a trivia question is never quite as much fun as the explanation, so there continue to be lots of anecdotes sprinkled throughout.

Having decided what the book was to be I began my list of lists. I had dozens and dozens of them everywhere, in my notebook, on scraps of paper and backs of envelopes, whenever I thought of one I jotted it down. I even took a micro-recorder in my pocket so I could take notes while driving. Then, when I had the skeleton for the book I started gathering information.

This was one undertaking I could not have completed alone. There were some topics I wanted to include which I felt I simply couldn't cover properly without a lot of help. So I called on some experts. You'll see their names as you read through the book.

It should be noted that others who contributed lists to this undertaking often indicated to me that their lists were not necessarily complete and that a fact or two may have been missed in preparing them. I know of instances where contributors pondered long and hard over their offerings; revising, adding and deleting. And contributors often mentioned that their personal lists may differ from lists compiled by other people with an interest in the same category. It's for that reason that in asking for someone's help in preparing this volume I would always ask for "significant" or "influential" events and people, rather than "the most important." One person may say that the most important event in Newfoundland aviation history would be the Arrow Air crash. Another may say the Alcock and Brown flight is paramount. Who's to say? Importance is purely subjective.

Aside from the listmakers whose names you will see in the book there are others who have contributed in vital ways—helping with research, suggestions, typing and so on. Here is my own list of people, without whom this book would have been an awful chore:

John O'Mara (CBC John that is... you'll encounter another John O'Mara later on), who has been a willing contributor to every book I've written; Eugene Howard, for advice; Kevin Collins of the Confederation Building Library; my co-workers Don Reynolds, Denise Wilson and Ted Blades; and, again, thanks to Liz Stanford of MUN's Inter-Library Loan department, who has managed to find many things that I thought were beyond finding.

So here it is, yet another Trivia Book. I hope it is worthy of a place on your flushbox.

Culture and Heritage

Where better to begin than with our own unique culture and heritage? Perhaps, to warm up, you will indulge me by considering a list of my favourite, original Newfoundland sayings:

A Newfoundland sealer once applied for a job at a factory. He said he needed the job because he had "lost his spring." The boss didn't know what he meant so he inquired of another Newfoundlander. The answer was that the sealer had gone out sealing with Captain Sam Blandford in the spring and had gotten no seals. This meant no wages that spring, hence he had "lost" his spring.

When was the last time you heard this term for boiling up: "storm the kettle." Of course, "boil up" and "have a mug up" are wonderful expressions as well.

Many years ago, a day when you got pork and cabbage for dinner was known as "Solomon Gosse's birthday." Two Solomon Gosses (Sr and Jr) were pioneer settlers of Torbay. It has been suggested that this saying was spread throughout Newfoundland in the early days of the seal hunt, when Torbaymen made up a large proportion of the crews.

Here are a few sayings I have come across which haven't been recorded anywhere else. Bill McCann is a co-worker of my brother Dennis at the provincial Department of Works, Services and Transportation. Bill is one of the funniest people I have ever met. He's got a witty saying for everything. One evening when I was in their company Bill and Dennis were discussing someone they knew. Bill's observation was that the man was "so off that if you put a level on his head you'd never find the bubble."

My uncle Will Bennett said he'd heard of a conductor on the Newfoundland Railway who had the following way of addressing his passengers: "All aboard for where you're goin'. All aboard for here, get out."

Harry Davis was the janitor at CBC in Gander when I worked there in the 1970s. (Matter of fact Harry was the janitor at half the businesses in Gander.) He was one of those truly nice people that everyone knew and liked, and the kind of man you remember all your life. I remember the change he carried in his pocket, which he would count every night. He carried so many coins he must have had reinforced pockets. I remember his colourful use of the English language. To Harry, we announcers at CBC worked, not in the control room, but in the "patrol" room. He talked about the benefits of using "profane" gas in your stove.

And if there was one area in which his language became especially colourful it was in a discussion of politics, particularly provincial politics. One night we were discussing the ability of a certain local politician to deal with the issues of the common man. Harry's comment was "He don't know no more about that than my arse knows about snipe shootin'." Bob Cuff offered a similar version from a Bay d'Espoir businessman who said, also speaking of a politician (oddly enough), "He knows no more about that than my arse knows about turr huntin'."

A couple of sayings became quite common about the time of the Cod Moratorium, partly because Buddy Wasisname and the Other Fellas used both in comedy sketches. The two sayings summed up the mindset of people who thought the Province was in deep trouble: "The arse is gone right out of 'er" and "she's gone b'y, she's gone." The first may even be a Kevin Blackmore original, but "she's gone b'y, she's gone" is a line from the climactic scene of the Tom Cahill play *As Loved Our Fathers*—and in that context refers the results of the second Confederation referendum.

When I sent a message to one of the Internet newsgroups asking for contributions of original Newfoundland sayings, Deborah Morrissey contributed the following. Although she said she didn't know who the author was, she felt it was cute. I've since heard other variations on it but Deborah's version was "I'm hungry enough to chew the arse off a low flying duck."

From the same newsgroup I got this response from Randy Follett who said "My friend, the late Patrick Connors, in response to complaints about the cold weather said 'Many are cold but few are frozen'."

A co-worker of my father's, when Dad worked at the Fire Department in St. John's, was Fred Holden. Captain Holden had the following philosophy of life which he espoused to many: "Fear God. Trust no man. And go your own way."

In the following three sayings, the language is a little stronger but I felt they should be written down for posterity. So be warned.

The reference to 'crooked' in the following saying refers to the man's temperament and not to anything larcenous. I heard the following in reference to someone that I knew. The man was said to be "so crooked that if he swallowed a nail, he'd shit a screw."

A bit of philosophy from a popular song in the 1980s got its own Newfoundland twist. By the way, for those of you not versed in the Newfoundland vernacular, 'What odds' means 'who cares.' In 1988, Bobby McFerrin recorded a number one pop song which offered the following bit of advice: "Don't Worry, Be Happy." It wasn't long before someone offered the Newfoundland version: "Shag it! What odds!"

This one is said to have happened during one of Joe Smallwood's election campaigns. It may be apocryphal, but it does make for a good line. Towards the end of his career as Premier, Smallwood was not meeting with the enthusiasm usually afforded him in previous campaigns. During one rally to a group of voters, Smallwood gave a speech in which he said something along the lines of "I love Newfoundland. I love this wonderful province of ours. I love Newfoundland so much if she were a woman I'd marry her." A voice in the back rejoindered "You might as well, you been screwing her long enough."

Ten early descriptions of Newfoundland and Labrador

1. 1527, John Rut: "all wilderness and mountaines and woodes, and no naturall ground but all mosse." From Rut's letter to Henry VII, written in St. John's harbour, which is the earliest first-hand English description of Newfoundland.
2. 1532, Jacques Cartier: "in fine, methinks it is the land God gave to Cain." An often-quoted description of the coast of Labrador.
3. 1583, Stephen Parmenius: "I ought to tell you about the customs, territories and inhabitants: but what shall I say when I see nothing but a very wilderness?" Parmenius was a Hungarian-born poet who accompanied Sir Humphrey Gilbert's expedition which claimed Newfoundland for England.
4. 1668, Merchants, Owners and Masters of the Western Ports: "the country is barren and rocky, is productive of no commodities as other Plantations, or affords anything of food to keep men alive."
5. 1675, a Mr. Perrot of Dartmouth, England (quoting a widespread saying at the time in the West of England): "If it were not for wood,

water and fish, Newfoundland were not worth a rush."
6. 1696, the Mayor of Plymouth: "for there is no land fit to be manured for to bring forth anything fit for the support for mankind."
7. 1698, Commodore Norris: "the Colony cannot subsist for it produces nothing. The country affords no subsistence to the planters."
8. 1768, Rev. Laurence Coughlan: "There are very few carpenters in Europe, who are able to hew a Piece of Timber with those in Newfoundland. They are a people of a very bright genius."
9. 1794, Aaron Thomas: "The Sky is generally overcast and a thick Fog fills the Atmosphere with a dismal, Cloudy and heavy mist which gives all living Creatures that move in it the appearance of heavyness of mind and the gait of sour sulleness."
10. 1827, Rev. William Bullock: "We love the place, O God" (The title of a hymn written for the consecration of St. Paul's Anglican church in Trinity, where Bullock was parish priest. It became one of the most popular hymns of all time.)

Perhaps Coughlan and Bullock, as men of the cloth, were more inclined to be charitable. But there is one other crucial difference between the two men of the cloth and the other detractors of Newfoundland: both Rev. Coughlan and Rev. Bullock actually lived here!

Perhaps the affections of Newfoundlanders for their Island home can be best summed up by an old joke: "How can you tell the Newfoundlanders from all other nations in the Kingdom of Heaven?—They're the ones chained to the wall, because all they really want from Paradise is to get back home." As Ray Guy once put it: "There is no other place."

Seven snappy comebacks

1. William F. Coaker: "Yes I am out of order, and if I wasn't I could piss ALL the way across." (After being declared out of order for stating in the House that he could piss halfway across the Long Bridge—which the government of the day was claiming as a major achievement of the administration.)
2. John Guppy: "I prefer to go out and fish." (John Guppy was a Labrador skipper elected MHA for Trinity in 1919. This was one of his very few utterances in the House. It was delivered in response to opposition taunts that he should be appointed Minister of Fisheries.)
3. Edward P. Morris: "What do I care for the Audit Act when the people are in need of bread?"

4. Robert Bond: "Tell him he is welcome to use it, as long as it does not leave the premises." (Responding to a request from a neighbour at Whitbourne that Bond loan him a lawnmower, after having received a similar response to an earlier request to borrow a book.)
5. Fannie McNeil: "I can bake bread AND vote as well!" (Responding to Sir Richard Squires, who suggested that she give up this "votes for women nonsense" and go home and bake bread.)
6. "Yes sir, will that be Ol or Nutting?" (housekeeper for doctors Nutting and Oliphant Fraser, when a drunken late-night caller insisted on "seeing the doctor.")
7. James Way: "Better beer in bigger bottles." (Way was Joe Smallwood's opponent in Bonavista North in the first provincial election. Way was responding to a question as to what he could promise to match "Joey's" pensions and baby bonus.)

Weather sayings

From time to time we'll still hear the famous "Red sky in the morning, sailors take warning. Red sky at night, sailor's delight." Here are a few sayings applied to the weather that you rarely, if ever, hear anymore.

1. A fine Christmas, a fat churchyard.
2. A warm Christmas, a cold Easter.
3. Clear moon, frost soon.
4. Rain before seven, lift before eleven.
5. When winds of October won't make the leaves go, then a frosty winter and banks of snow.
6. Winter thunder means summer hunger.
7. If Candlemas Day be fair and fine, half the winter is left behind.
8. If the wind's in the east on Candlemas Day, there it will stick till the first of May.
9. Evening red and morning grey, double signs of one fine day.
10. Sea birds keeping near the land, tell a storm is near at hand. But flying seaward out of sight, you may stay and fish all night.

Ice conditions

The Newfoundland climate has been known to strain the Queen's English in new and exciting directions. Here is a list of some of the many Newfoundland words used to describe different ice conditions — approximately arranged from freeze-up to break-up.

greasy waters
sish
local ice
copy pans
rough ice
bergy waters
rough ice
ice islands
rotten ice

pancake ice
slob
swatchy ice
ballicatters
growlers
bergy bits
icebergs
sandy ice

"Quare ice" is another great Newfoundland term, referring to flowing water that has frozen.

Ten Beothuk words

Widdun - Asleep
Wasemook - Salmon
Tapaithook - Canoe
Buggishaman - White Man
Shannok - Micmac Indians
Thudwed - Dancing
Suauthou - Singing
Monau - Seals
Boochauwit - I am hungry
Gosset - Beothuk country of the dead

If anyone is ever looking for an unusual name for a newborn, here are two suggestions from the Beothuk language: *Bobosheret* (codfish) and *Shaudaume* (partridgeberry).

Three uses for a haddock

Years ago, proper application of this fish was considered a great cure for any number of ills.

1. To cure rheumatic pains, carry a haddock bone in your pocket.
2. To cure a toothache, remove the fin bone of a haddock (while the fish is still alive) and wear the bone in a bag around your neck.
3. To cure cramps, use the fin of a haddock. It was important that the fish must not have touched the outside of the boat or the gangboards.

Heritage buildings

In years past most people did not place much importance on the significance that various buildings, sites and monuments had in defining who we were as a culture. Shane O'Dea has perhaps done as much as any one person to help remedy this. He also assisted me by compiling the following heritage building lists. First, 28 significant heritage buildings in the Province:

The Roman Catholic Basilica of St. John the Baptist in St. John's
The Anglican Cathedral of St. John the Baptist in St. John's
Government House, St. John's
The Colonial Building, St. John's
Commissariat House, St. John's
Devon Place, St. John's (now the Captain's Quarters Hotel, on Kingsbridge Road)
The Court House, Harbour Grace
Ryan's Shop, Trinity
The Ryan Premises, Bonavista
Alexander (Bridge) House, Bonavista
St. Paul's Church, Trinity
Roman Catholic Church, Trinity
The Young House, Upper Island Cove
The Moravian Mission House and its adjacent complex, Hopedale, Labrador
The Slade/Baine Johnston/Earle Premises, Battle Harbour, Labrador
St. Paul's Church, Harbour Grace
St Peter's Church, Twillingate
Grand Falls House
Bleak House, Fogo
Rorke's Stone Jug, Carbonear
The Railway Station, St. John's
St. Patrick's Church, St. John's
Presentation Convent and School, St. John's
Mallard Cottage, Quidi Vidi
The Customs House (Museum), Harbour Grace
Ridley Hall, Harbour Grace
Ridley Offices, Harbour Grace
Cabot Tower

Threatened heritage structures

Time, the elements and neglect have taken their toll on many structures closely linked to our heritage. Here is a list of five

15

architectural treasures that have been allowed to deteriorate to the point where they are threatened with demolition or collapse.

Alexander House, Bonavista
Ridley Hall, Harbour Grace
Ridley Offices, Harbour Grace
The Marshall Building, Water Street, St. John's (This building was torn down as this book was being prepared for print.)
The Moravian complex, Hopedale

Lost treasures of Newfoundland architecture

1. The Earle Premises, Fogo. The most significant collection of fishery buildings that had survived into the 1980s. The many buildings that made up Earle's Room dated from 1815 to about 1913.
2. The *Gazette* Building, Water Street at McBrides Hill, St. John's. The finest and most elaborate of the commercial buildings built on Water Street after the Great Fire of 1892, this building was demolished in the 1960s to make way for the Bank of Montreal.
3. The Carter House, Carter's Hill, St. John's. This was quite possibly the birthplace of Prime Minister Frederick Carter. Built on the site in 1816, it had much of its original interior into the 1970s. It was demolished around 1982.
4. Winterton, Winter Avenue, St. John's. Built around 1809, this was the ancestral home of the Winter family. It was owned by the Furlong family from about 1910, and was the home of retired Chief Justice Robert Furlong when it burned down in 1996. The elderly former Chief Justice also died in the fire, while conservators have yet to determine just how much of Furlong's unparalleled collection of Newfoundlandia was also damaged beyond recovery.
5. Ayre & Sons, Water Street, St. John's. One of a great range of buildings that determined the character of the south side of that section of Water Street. The building was demolished in 1972 to make way for Atlantic Place.
6. Blenheim House, Placentia. This was the home of the Sweetman family from Waterford, Ireland—for many years the principal merchant house of Placentia Bay. The house was built around 1786 and demolished in the 1930s. It was very finely furnished in the Adam style and may have had Prince William Henry as a guest when he was surrogate in Placentia in 1786.
7. Bailey House, Oderin, Placentia Bay. The home was built by Nelson Collingwood Bailey, a clerk to the historic Spurrier firm, in 1834. A very good example of the Newfoundland vernacular house, it was

demolished around 1990.
8. Cramp's Farm, Freshwater Road, St. John's. This single-story, settle fireplace, full-studded house was the last surviving example of this type in St. John's. It was demolished around 1994.
9. The Pike House, Carbonear. This house was built around 1824 and was an extended version of the typical planter's house of the period. It is thought by many to have been the house of Sheila Nageira—the "Irish Princess" who married Gilbert Pike—but this is erroneous, as she died 200 years before the house was built. There was probably an earlier Pike house on the site, as suggested by a grave in the garden. The Pike House was demolished in the 1980s.

Newfoundland "survivals"

What follows is a list of "heritage items" which have been preserved in Newfoundland, in part because of our isolation.

1. Newfoundland English. With all its dialects, idioms and expressions, the study of Newfoundland English is a folklorist's dream come true.
2. French folklore/speech. Despite outside influences the French language is spoken and French culture still thrives in many areas of Newfoundland and Labrador, most notably in the Port au Port Peninsula, the St. George's Bay area and the Codroy Valley.
3. L'anse aux Meadows. A remarkable archaeological find in that it gave evidence that the Vikings had lived here around the year 1000. In 1968 it was declared a National Historic Park, and a World Heritage Site in 1978.
4. The L'anse Armour burial mound. The Labrador Straits is the location of the earliest verified site of human habitation in the Province. The burial mound there has been dated to about 5000 B.C., and has been described as the oldest human burial of this complexity anywhere in the world.
5. Dorset Eskimo sites. Evidence of the Dorset Eskimo culture have been found at the Beaches and Shamblers' Cove in Bonavista Bay, but the best known site is at Port aux Choix where a National Historic Site has been established.
6. Christmas mumming. An ancient English custom that is still practised only in Newfoundland. ("Jannying" is against the law, believe it or not. In 1972 when the Mummer's Troupe was founded one of their aims was to travel around St. John's dressed in mummer's garb, dropping into this house and that one. The group received a friendly phone call from the gendarmes informing them that if they

were to do so they'd be breaking the law.)
7. Spruce beer. Originally brewed in the 1600s, it was the most common beverage drunk by fishermen and labourers in the 18th and 19th centuries. It is still available in stores.
8. Hard tack. Around since the 17th century when it was widely used by European mariners and armies in the field (known as ship's biscuit, pilot biscuit or Hamburg bread), hard tack remains the unique ingredient in the cooking of Fish and Brewis. There are several methods of preparing our "national dish," some using fresh cod, others using salt cod, but always with hard bread. Hard tack is also commonly given to infants as a "teething biscuit!"

Two things you probably thought were Newfoundlandia but aren't:

1. Reddi Kilowatt. At one time whenever you saw an ad for Newfoundland Light and Power, you saw their spokesman, a stick-like figure named Reddi Kilowatt, and many of us thought he was Newfoundland Light and Power invention. Not so, in fact he was the symbol for many power companies in North America. Reddi was invented by Ashton Collins who ran Reddi Communications of Greenwich, Connecticut. Newfoundland Light and Power subscribed to the Reddi Communications service which included a large database of electrical info and got Reddi in the bargain. An interesting bit of Newfoundlandia associated with Reddi Kilowatt concerns the New Democratic Party. When the party was being established in Newfoundland it decided to make the power company one of its targets in a fight against the profits made by huge corporations. They ran an ad which showed a picture of Reddi Kilowatt and alongside a caption which read "You'd smile too if you made 14 million dollars last year." Newfoundland Light and Power decided to take legal action and stop the ads. They got nowhere. By this time Reddi Kilowatt was in the public domain.
2. Chuck Connors. Of all the show business personalities who may or may not have been from Newfoundland, Chuck Connors can create more arguments than anyone else. Sorry, folks. Chuck Connors was born in Brooklyn, New York. However, all is not lost, his mother was a Lundrigan from Peters River, St. Mary's Bay. His father was from Placentia.

Favourite tipples

The most popular alcoholic beverages in Newfoundland and

Labrador, as of August 1996 according to the Newfoundland Liquor Corporation. (Thank you to Fraser Lush and Sharon Jeans.)

White Rum	1. Bacardi White
	2. Captain Morgan White
Light Rum	1. Lamb's Palm Breeze
	2. Bacardi Amber
Dark Rum	1. Captain Morgan Black
	2. Screech
Canadian Whiskey	1. Golden Wedding
	2. Seagram's Five Star
Scotch Whiskey	1. Bell's Extra Special
	2. Johnny Walker Red
Other Whiskey	1. Jack Daniels
	2. Jamesons Irish
Gin	1. Gordon's Dry
	2. Gilbey Dry
Vodka	1. Smirnoff
	2. Russian Prince
Liqueurs	1. Kahlua
	2. Bailey's Irish Cream
Brandy	1. Charenac
	2. D'Eaubonne
Fortified Wine	1. Hermit Sherry
	2. Old Niagara Port
Sparkling Wine	1. Bright's Spumante Bambino
	2. Cartier Spumante Bianco
White Wine	1. Le Piat D'Or White
	2. B & G Parteger White
Red Wine	1. Markland Blueberry
	2. Markland Partridgeberry
Imported Beer	1. Corona Extra
	2. Heineken

Newfoundland's ten rarest coins

Thanks to John O'Mara of Cardboard Heroes on Duckworth Street for supplying this information. The coins are listed along with approximate values (good-uncirculated).

1. 1845, Peter M'Auslane farthing ($1500-$3000).
2. 1871(H), ten cent ($3000-$10,000).

3. 1873(H), five cent ($700-$5000).
4. 1880, two dollar gold ($1000-$5000).
5. 1870, ten cent ($250-$10,000).
6. 1858, ship ha'penny ($200-$1250).
7. 1880 (oval "0"), penny ($150-$3000).
8. 1885, ten cent ($100-$7500).
9. 1872, two dollar gold ($375-$12,500).
10. 1946, five cent ($375-$4000).

Politics and Government

The Prime Ministers of Newfoundland

Philip Little (1855-1858)
John Kent (1858-1861)
Hugh W. Hoyles (1861-1865)
Frederick B.T. Carter (1865-1869 & 1874-1878)
Charles J.F. Bennett (1870-1874)
William V. Whiteway (1878-1885, 1889-1894, 1895-1897)
Robert Thorburn (1885-1889)
Augustus F. Goodridge (11 Apr-12 Dec, 1894)
Daniel J. Greene (13 Dec 1894-8 Feb 1895)
James S. Winter (1897-1900)
Robert Bond (1900-1909)
Edwards P. Morris (1909-1917)
William F. Lloyd (Jan 1918-May 1919)
Michael P. Cashin (May-Nov, 1919)
Richard A. Squires (1919-1923 & 1928-1932)
William R. Warren (Jul 1923-Apr 1924)
Albert E. Hickman (10 May-11 June 1924)
Walter S. Monroe (1924-1928)
Frederick A. C. Alderdice (1928, 1932-1934)

The terms Premier and Prime Minister were used interchangeably in the nineteenth century, with "premier" being the more usual. Sir Edward P. Morris was the first to insist upon the use of the term Prime Minister for the office.

There were no Prime Ministers between 1934 and 1949. Responsible government was suspended and Commission of Government was instituted on February 16, 1934 under the chairmanship of Governor Sir David Murray Anderson. The first six commissioners were Frederick Alderdice, William R. Howley, and John C. Puddester from Newfoundland; Sir John Hope Simpson, E.N.R. Trentham, and Thomas Lodge from Britain.

Newfoundland saw its next premier in 1949 with the election of J.R. Smallwood.

Premiers of Newfoundland

>Joseph R. Smallwood (1949-1972)
>Frank D. Moores (1972-1979)
>A. Brian Peckford (1979-1989)
>Thomas G. Rideout (Mar. 21-May 5, 1989)
>Clyde K. Wells (1989-1996)
>Brian Tobin (1996-)

Early Governors of Newfoundland

>Cupids: John Guy (1610-1615).
>Cupids: John Mason (1615-1621).
>Bristol's Hope: Robert Hayman (1618-1628).
>Aquaforte-Renews: Richard Whitbourne (1618-1620).
>South Falkland: Francis Tanfield (1623-1625).
>Avalon: Edward Wynne (1621-1625).
>Avalon: Arthur Aston (1626-1627).
>Avalon: George Calvert, Lord Baltimore (1626-1627).
>Avalon: Unknown (1629-1634).
>Avalon: William Hill (1634-1638).
>All of Newfoundland: David Kirke (1638-1651).
>All of Newfoundland: John Treworgie (1652-1660).

French Governors at Plaisance

>1655: Sieur de Kereon (appointed but did not serve).
>1660: Nicholas Gargot (appointed but did not serve).
>1662: Thalour du Perron.
>1664: Bellot.
>1667: La Palme.
>1670: La Poippe.
>1685: Antoine Parat.

1690: Louis de Pastour de Costebelle (interim).
1691: Jacques-Francois de Mombeton de Brouillan,
1702: Daniel d'Auger de Subercase.
1706: Phillippe de Pastour de Costebelle.

After the signing of the Treaty of Utrecht in 1713 the British renamed Plaisance "Placentia," and appointed John Moody its Lieutenant-Governor. Both Moody and his successor, Samuel Gledhill, were responsible to the Governor of Nova Scotia.

Naval Governors of Newfoundland

1729-30: Henry Osborne.
1731: George Clinton.
1732: Edward Falkingham.
1733-34: Robert McCarthy, Viscount Muskerry.
1735-37: FitzRoy Henry Lee.
1738: Philip Vanbrugh.
1739-40: Henry Medley.
1740: George Graham.
1741: Thomas Smith (first term).
1742: John Byng.
1743: Thomas Smith (second term).
1744: Charles Hardy.
1745: Richard Edwards.
1746-47: none.
1748: Charles Watson.
1749: George B. Rodney.
1750-52: Francis William Drake.
1753-54: Hugh Bonfoy.
1755-56: Richard Dorrill.
1757-59: Richard Edwards (first term).
1760: James Webb.
1761-63: Thomas Graves.
1764-68: Hugh Palliser.
1769-71: John Byron.
1772-74: Molyneux Shuldham.
1775: Richard Duff.
1776-78: John Montagu.
1779-81: Richard Edwards (second term).
1782-85: John Campbell.
1786-88: John Elliott.

1789-91: Mark Milbanke.
1792-93: Richard King.
1794-96: James Wallace.
1797-99: William Waldegrave.
1800-01: Charles M. Pole.
1802-03: James Gambier.
1804-06: Erasmus Gower.
1807-09: John Holloway.
1810-12: John T. Duckworth.
1813-15: Richard G. Keats.
1816-17: Francis Pickmore (the first Governor to winter in Newfoundland).
1818-24: Charles Hamilton (the first Governor to *survive* a winter in Newfoundland).

Resident Governors of Newfoundland (appointed after Newfoundland received colonial status)

1825-34 Thomas J. Cochrane.
1835-41 Henry Prescott.
1841-46 John Harvey.
1847-52 John G. LeMarchant.
1852-55 Ker Baillie Hamilton.
1855-57 Charles H. Darling.
1857-64 Alexander Bannerman.
1864-69 Anthony Musgrave.
1869-76 Stephen John Hill.
1876-80 John Hawley Glover (first term).
1881-83 Henry F. Maxse.
1884-85 John Hawley Glover (second term).
1886-87 George W. DesVoeux.
1887-89 Henry A. Blake.
1889-95 Terence N. O'Brien.
1896-98 Herbert H. Murray.
1898-01 Henry E. McCallum.
1901-04 Cavendish Boyle.
1904-09 William MacGregor.
1909-13 Ralph C. Williams.
1913-17 Walter E. Davidson.
1917-22 Charles A. Harris.

1922-28 William L Allardyce.
1928-32 John Middleton.
1932-36 David Murray Anderson.
1936-46 Humphrey T. Walwyn.
1946-49 Gordon MacDonald.

Newfoundland communities re-named after colonial governors

1. Musgravetown (formerly Goose Bay, Bonavista Bay) & Musgrave Harbour (formerly Muddy Hole).
2. Glovertown (formerly Bloody Bay) & Glover's Harbour (formerly Thimble Tickles).
3. Blaketown (formerly Dildo Pond—although there is a tradition that the name was a contraction of "By-the-Lake-Town).
4. Terrenceville (formerly Head of Fortune Bay). By this time it had become established tradition to name a community after the Governor. Governor O'Brien was the first to have a community named for his Christian name, although the Governor spelled his name with one "r." The tradition apparently died on the vine with his successor, Governor Murray, who made himself unpopular with the politicians of the day.
5. McCallum (formerly Bonne Bay).
6. Cavendish (formerly Broad Cove, Trinity Bay—renamed in honour of Governor Boyle).
7. Williamsport (formerly Greenspond, White Bay) and Champneys (formerly Salmon Cove, Trinity Bay). Governor Ralph Champneys Williams was the only Governor to have a community renamed in honour of his *middle* name.

By contrast, only three communities were named after Prime Ministers: Winterton (formerly Scilly Cove, Trinity Bay), Whiteway (Witless Bay, Trinity Bay) and Morrisville (Lynch's Cove, Bay d'Espoir). Port Hope Simpson, Labrador was named in honour of Commissioner Sir John Hope Simpson.

Lieutenant-Governors of Newfoundland and Labrador

1949: Albert Walsh.
1949-57: Leonard Outerbridge.
1957-63: Campbell MacPherson.

1963-68: Fabian O'Dea.
1968-74: E. John A. Harnum.
1974-81: Gordon A. Winter.
1981-86: Anthony W. Paddon.
1986-91: James McGrath.
1991- : Frederick W. Russell.

As of this writing a successor to Lieutenant-Governor Russell has not been named.

Twenty politicians, first elected to office under the age of 30

1. John Slade (23) - MHA Twillingate, 1842.
2. Bill Rowe (24) - MHA White Bay South, 1966.
3. Kevin Aylward (24) - MHA Stephenville, 1985.
4. Brian Tobin (25) - MP Humber/St. George's/St. Barbe, 1980.
5. Richard Cashin (25) - MP St. John's East, 1962.
6. Robert Bond (25) - MHA Trinity Bay, 1882.
7. James A. McGrath (25) - MP St. John's East, 1957.
8. John Henry Scammell (25) - MHA St. Barbe, 1919.
9. Edward Patrick Morris (26) - MHA St. John's West, 1885.
10. Ed Roberts (26) - MHA White Bay North, 1966.
11. John Kent (27) - MHA St. John's West, 1832.
12. Fonse Faour (27) - MP Humber/St. George's/St. Barbe, 1978.
13. John T. Cheeseman (27) - MHA Burin, 1919.
14. Tom Rideout (27) - MHA Baie Verte/White Bay, 1975.
15. Philip Francis Little (28) - MHA St. John's, 1852. (Little became Prime Minister of Newfoundland at age 31).
16. Bill Smallwood (28) - MHA Green Bay, 1966.
17. Michael Cashin (29) - MHA Ferryland, 1893.
18. John Lundrigan (29) - MP Gander/Twillingate, 1968.
19. Charles Power (29) - MHA Ferryland, 1977.
20. Gene Long (29) - MHA St. John's East, 1986.

Ten resounding election victories

1. *1966*: The Liberals take 39 of 42 seats. Joey was riding a crest of popularity with the start-up of the Churchill Falls power project, the completion of the Trans Canada Highway the year before, and lowering the voting age from 21 to 19. In the election PC leader Noel Murphy was defeated in Humber East by Clyde Wells. This election

marked the last in a series of six overwhelming victories for Smallwood: 1949, 1951, 1956, 1959, and 1961. After Confederation, virtually every provincial riding off the Avalon Peninsula was a safe Liberal Seat for 20 years.

2. *1951*: John R. Courage took 96% of the popular vote in the district of Fortune Hermitage for the Liberals. A popular teacher contesting his home district, Courage was appointed deputy speaker and later became the second speaker of the House of Assembly.

3. *1882*: Whiteway supporter Captain Charles Dawe was marked on almost 94% of the ballots cast in the two-member district of Harbour Grace. This was one year after a beginning had been made on the Newfoundland Railway. The proposed terminus for first stage in the construction was Harbour Grace. In that general election the Whiteway Party won 26 of 33 seats, over the New Party. Dawe's running mate Ambrose Shea had picked up the nickname 'Oily Gammon' from their New Party opponents, while Captain Dawe was known as his 'Lacky Charlie'—but apparently without suffering any ill effects at the polls.

4. *1900*: Robert Bond's Liberal Party takes 32 of 36 seats. The chief issue is opposition to the 1898 Railway contract, and A.B. Morine's Conservatives are not helped by the fact that the electorate identifies them as being in league with the Reid Newfoundland Company.

5. *1949*: Reginald F. Sparkes wins 93% of the popular vote in St. Barbe (where he had been a schools inspector for many years prior to Confederation). Sparkes was appointed the first speaker of the Provincial House of Assembly.

6. *1957*: Chesley Carter is elected Member of Parliament for Burgeo/LaPoile by acclamation, the only MP ever to have been so elected in Newfoundland and Labrador. In two previous elections he had polled 92% and 88% of the popular vote in the most strongly Confederate part of the Province.

7. *1932*: Frederick C. Alderdice's United Newfoundland Party wins 24 of 27 seats, as the country rises up against a corrupt Squires government in the depths of the Great Depression. Liberal Joseph R. Smallwood is soundly defeated in Bonavista South.

8. *1965*: The Liberals sweep of all seven federal seats (repeating their sweep of 1963) helping re-elect Lester Pearson with the slogan "We'll finish the drive in '65, thanks to Mr. Pearson" (referring to the completion of the Trans Canada Highway across the Province).

9. *1993*: The Liberals again sweep all seven federal seats, as Newfoundland joins in a rejection of the Conservative government.

10. *1968*: Six of the seven federal seats go to the Progressive Conser-

vatives as Newfoundland voters rebel against Mr. Smallwood and reject the Trudeaumania which swept across most of the country. Don Jamieson was the lone Liberal to stem the Tory tide.

Ten political characters

1. Thomas Fitzgibbon Moore. An eccentric, Moore would to walk from his home in Dildo to attend sessions of the House of Assembly while MHA of Trinity, 1836-37. A true frontier "character" Moore cared little for the turned-up noses of the St. John's merchants forced to sit beside him in the House.
2. Hughie Shea. A St. John's grocer at the time, Shea made an unsuccessful run at the leadership of the PC Party in 1970. He ran in the 1971 election and took St. John's South for the PCs. When Premier Frank Moores appointed his cabinet Shea wasn't among the chosen. In response he crossed the House to sit as an independent. In 1972, Shea and Tom Burgess created a political tempest, as they held the balance of power in the House of Assembly and both Liberals and Tories vied for their support. In the 1972 General Election both Burgess and Shea lost. Shea later wrote a book called *Shea's Newfoundland Seduced* which gave his interpretation of Newfoundland's problems (a volume of his poetry was also published after his death). Hughie Shea was perhaps equally well-known for his choice of names for two of his business enterprises: a convenience store called "Shea's Rip-Off" and a fast food outlet known as "Hamburger Hell." Hughie Shea died in 1993.
3. Alfred B. Morine. A Nova Scotian-born politician who was described by Sir James Winter as "the biggest scoundrel ever to have come in through the Narrows," Morine coined the expression that Newfoundlanders were "too green to burn." He was also responsible for the infamous "Greenspond Letter" which intimated that a political foe was having sexual relations with a woman in Greenspond who had a venereal disease.
4. Dorothy Wyatt. The first woman elected to St. John's City Council, she became mayor in 1973. Instantly recognizable because of her flamboyant wardrobe and her outspoken manner, she was one politician who had no problem living up to her campaign slogan: "Vote for Wyatt—She won't be quiet." As mayor of St. John's she had a special telephone line, which she called the "Dotline," installed in her office at City Hall to make it easier for taxpayers to contact her.
5. Stephen March. March was a merchant from Old Perlican, Trinity Bay who sat for two terms as an MHA. March was full of far-

fetched schemes including an effort to erect an arch across the Narrows in the 1861 to welcome Royal visitors to the country, an attempt to colonize Funk Island and building of stone fences in order to get the country moving again (warning, "Newfoundland will never prosper without it!").

6. John Crosbie. A true political character, John Crosbie is articulate, outspoken, witty and never afraid of controversy. His clashes with Liberal Sheila Copps in the House of Commons were legendary. Knowing this it was hilarious to hear the two play the lovers Rick and Ilsa in an adaptation of the great love story "Casablanca" for CBC Radio's Morningside program.

7. Ron Pumphrey. "Hello, m'lovelies" was Pumphrey's introduction on his popular VOCM call-in show in the 1970s. He also recorded a couple of comedy albums, one of which was called "Ha! So Ya Sleep on Your Belly Do Ya, Eh, Baby?!" In 1981 he was elected to St. John's city council, promising to "put a heart in city hall." Ron left politics to become a Salvation Army officer, but resigned his commission and returned to the airwaves in 1989.

8. Oliver L. Vardy. Vardy moved to the U.S. from Newfoundland at an early age. Before returning home in the thirties, he had served a term in prison for armed robbery. He entered provincial politics in 1949, after he had served as a St. John's city councillor. In the 1970s, after Frank Moores' Conservatives came to power, Vardy was shown to have used his position for personal financial gain. He escaped to Panama, then to Florida, where he managed to fight extradition until his death in 1980.

9. Peter Brennan. Brennan was a bonesetter by trade, so successful that he ended up owning a choice piece of property in downtown St. John's. He was elected to represent St. John's West in 1866 at the age of 80, making him in all likelihood the oldest person ever elected to the House of Assembly. (Certainly the oldest rookie MHA, in any case!) After Brennan died in April 1887, all his possessions were willed to the Roman Catholic church. He was buried at Belvedere cemetery in St. John's where an elaborate headstone proclaimed him a "centenarian and a celibate."

10. Rossie Barbour. Always a bridesmaid but never a bride, Rossie Barbour never held a cabinet post in the Smallwood government, but he was a true constituent politician and served his district faithfully until his defeat (along with many other strong Liberals) in the 1972 general election. He was known both for the blunt manner in which he approached the issues and his unique construction of the Queen's English.

Eight politicians in the wrong profession

1. Ted Russell (writer). Best known as the creator of "the Chronicles of Uncle Mose," Russell served for a time as a member of Smallwood's cabinet, until a disagreement with the Premier caused him to resign.
2. Harold Horwood (writer). Another of Smallwood's supporters who left the fold after disagreements with the Premier, Horwood turned to journalism and became one of Smallwood's harshest critics. Still later he became known as a novelist and nature writer.
3. Michael Kearney (shipwright) - Perhaps Newfoundland's best-known shipbuilder from the Golden Age of Sail, Kearney served one term in the House of Assembly from 1865 to 1869. His reputation as a naval architect was such that he was called in to assist in the construction of the *Great Eastern*.
4. Abram Kean (sealer). The most successful seal hunter in Newfoundland history, Kean ran for political office and won quite easily, even though by his own admission he had been "pitchforked into a position which I neither sought nor desired."
5. Daniel W. Prowse (historian/judge). Elected to the House in 1861, Prowse later gained greater fame as a great jurist and historian. He could also rate as one of our characters in that, during his tenure as a circuit judge, he thought nothing of having poachers who were awaiting trial accompany him on his own hunting expeditions for partridge and snipe.
6. Thomas Talbot (author/educator). Although he served several terms as a member of the House of Assembly, it was as a scholar that Talbot excelled. He wrote novels, essays, and poetry, and taught at St. Bonaventure's College for many years.
7. John Delaney (postmaster). Delaney served in the House of Assembly for a number of years but gave up shortly after being appointed postmaster general in 1860. He was also Newfoundland's first meteorologist, having set up an observing station at his home in St. John's.
8. Patrick Kough (builder). Serving in the first House of Assembly in Newfoundland as a member for St. John's, Kough was appointed superintendent of public buildings in 1834. He soon found himself in disfavour with the hierarchy of the Roman Catholic Church in St. John's who accused him of being in cahoots with protestant merchants. Kough decided not to run in the 1836 election and turned his attention instead to building construction. After finding favour again with the RC Church he worked on the Roman Catholic

Cathedral and Presentation Convent, and in later years the Colonial Building and his own farm on the outskirts of the city.

Ten women who ran for public office

1. Julia Salter Earle, a well known suffragette and labour leader, ran for St. John's municipal council in 1925. She and two other female candidates were defeated, although Salter Earle missed by only a handful of votes. After the election there was some question about the misplacing of a ballot box and other irregularities. Although she was encouraged to seek a recount, Earle refused.
2. Lady Helena Squires, the wife of Prime Minister Sir Richard Squires, was the first woman to seek election to the Newfoundland House of Assembly. Lady Squires was successful in a by-election in 1930 in the district of Lewisporte. She lost her seat in 1932. (It is ironic that during Sir Richard's first term in office in 1919 to 1923, both he and Lady Helena opposed giving women the vote).
3. Martha Hann was the only woman to run in the June 1946 election to select delegates to attend the National Convention. Hann was defeated in Humber District.
4. Grace Sparkes ran in four elections. In the 1949 and 1951 provincial elections she ran in Burin district and in the Federal elections of 1949 and 1953 she ran in Burin-Burgeo. She was defeated each time. No other woman ran in a federal election until 1963 when Edna Murphy ran and was defeated in Humber-St. Georges.
5. Blanche (Blackie) Drover was the first woman elected to a municipal council in Newfoundland. Drover was elected in 1957, receiving more votes than any of the eight men who had run for office in Clarenville. By tradition she should have been selected mayor, but the job was given to former mayor Boyce Smith. A number of voters submitted a petition protesting against the selection. Mayor Smith and five other councillors resigned and Drover was chosen as the new mayor, becoming the first woman in Newfoundland history to hold the post. However the Minister of Municipal Affairs declared the election null and void because nomination day in the town had been postponed when only two people had offered themselves for election. Even though the same thing had happened in other communities with no intervention by the provincial government, a new election was called for Clarenville alone. The council was dismissed and, when ballots were cast for a second election, Drover came sixth. She had served a total of 35 days as mayor.
6. Jean Fowlow was elected to the Stephenville council in 1961. She

again sought and was successful in getting a council seat in 1965, 1969, 1973, and 1977. She was selected as the town's mayor in 1969 and held the post until 1974. Although she polled more votes than anyone else in the 1977 election, she declined when asked to be mayor again.
7. Dorothy Wyatt became the first woman elected to St. John's city council in 1969. In 1973 she was elected mayor. Businesswoman Hazel Newhook also elected mayor of Gander in 1973.
8. Hazel MacIsaac became the first female Member of the House of Assembly since Confederation when she took the district of St. George's for the Liberals in 1975. The 1975 election also saw five other female candidates: Averill Baker (Gander), Helen Porter (Mount Pearl), Esther Spracklin (Grand Bank), Marlene Maynard (Strait of Belle Isle) and Elizabeth Genge (Waterford-Kenmount). Only MacIsaac was successful.
9. Hazel Newhook (Gander) and Lynn Verge (Humber East) were successful in the 1979 provincial election, which saw 15 female candidates. Hazel MacIsaac was defeated. Both Newhook and Verge received cabinet posts, making them the first female Ministers in Newfoundland history. Newhook and Verge were re-elected in 1982, making them the first two Newfoundland women to have crossed that political threshold.
10. Bonnie Hickey and Jean Payne became the first female Members of Parliament from Newfoundland when they were successful in the 1993 Federal Election.

Longest service on municipal council

1. Baxter Gillard, Englee (34 years, included four years appointed).
2. Edward Sheaves, Port Aux Basques (33 years).
3. Caleb Ackerman, Glovertown (32 years).
4. Joseph Ollerhead, St. Anthony (31 years).
5. William Hibbs, Peterview (28 years).
5. Karl Hiscock, Labrador City (28 years).
7. Bernard Finlay, St. Shotts (27 years).
8. Elmer Bursey, Botwood, (26 years).
9. Jack Curlew, Lewisporte (25 years).
9. Kevin Walsh, Stephenville (25 years).
9. Cecil Winsor, Wesleyville (25 years).
9. Ancel Duffitt, Catalina (25 years).
9. Sandy Payne, Ramea (25 years).
14. Harvey Hodder, Mount Pearl (24 years).
14. James Fagan, St. John's (24 years).

Longest service in federal or provincial politics

1. *54 years*—Sir Edward Dalton Shea (10 years as Member of the House of Assembly, 44 years as Member of the Legislative Council). Shea was originally elected as a supporter of our first Prime Minister, Philip Lewis, in 1855. Just before his death in 1913 he was honoured as the senior active legislator in the British Empire.
2. *37 years*—Dr. George Skelton (seven years as MHA, 30 as MLC).
3. *36 years*—Fred Rowe (20 as MHA, 16 as Senator), holder of the post-Confederation record.
4. *35 years*—Robert John Parsons (all as MHA for St. John's East).
5. *35 years*—John Kent (29 as MHA, six as MLC).
6. *33 years*—Ambrose Shea (held five different seats). With his brother Edward, a combined 87 years in Newfoundland politics!
7. *33 years*—Edward P. Morris (as MHA for St. John's West).
8. *31 years*—Sir Robert Bond.
9. *31 years*—Sir Michael Cashin.
10. *31 years*—William J. Woodford.

Honourable mentions:

James McGrath (24 years as MP), longest service in federal politics and longest-serving Tory.

John Crosbie served 27 years in total, federal and provincial, six as a Liberal or Independent Liberal.

Pat Canning (27 years), longest-serving post-Confederation MHA.

Lynn Verge (18 years), longest serving woman.

Gerry Ottenheimer is the longest-serving active politician. He spent 20 years in the House of Assembly between 1966 and 1988 (he was out of politics during 1969-1971) and was appointed to the Senate in 1988.

Districts which supported Confederation by more than 3-1 in the second referendum of 1948

1. Burgeo LaPoile (89% in favour of Confederation).
2. Burin (81%).
3. Fortune Hermitage (80%). The three South Coast districts had a long tradition of family and economic ties with Nova Scotia and were also overwhelmingly Protestant.
4. St. Barbe (79%).
5. Labrador (77%).

6. White Bay (76%).
7. Twillingate (75%).
8. Bonavista North (75%).

Districts which supported Responsible Government in the 1948 referendum

1. Ferryland (85%).
2. Harbour Main-Bell Island (83%).
3. Placentia and St. Mary's (82%). The three overwhelmingly Roman Catholic districts.
4. St. John's East (69%).
5. St. John's West (67%). The two St. John's Districts were by far the most populous. Although Confederation carried the Island apart from the Avalon Peninsula (as well as Labrador) the anti-Confederate vote in St. John's was enough to make the overall outcome very close.
6. Harbour Grace (62%).
7. Port De Grave (51%). This was the closest race in the referendum. Bonavista South voted for Confederation by a slightly greater margin.

Hardest-fought election campaigns

1. The 1948 Confederation Referenda.
2. The 1971 Provincial election. On election night the standings were 21 PCs, 20 Liberals, one New Labrador Party. Notable in particular for the Sallys Cove incident in St. Barbe South, in which a ballot box went missing. It was later learned that the returning officer had accidentally burned the ballots. Seven seats were decided by less than 100 votes: Bay de Verde, Burgeo, Carbonear, Ferryland, St. Mary's, St. Barbe and Labrador South.
3. The Tie Election of 1908—18 seats for the People's Party of Sir Edward Morris and 18 for Sir Robert Bond's Liberals. In Harbour Main, 15 more votes for the Liberal candidate would have changed the result, while People's Party candidate A.H. Seymour lost Harbour Grace by only three votes.
4. The McLea Election of 1861. The campaign and polling day were marked by violence and threats of violence. In St. John's West Conservative Kenneth M'Lea withdrew after his business premises were vandalized. A blockade at the Cat's Cove polling station turned ugly and resulted in the death of one man. And in Harbour Grace the fear of violence was so great that the magistrates there refused

to open the polls, so there was no return. Result: 14 Conservatives, 12 Liberals, two vacant. When the House opened there was a full-fledged riot, which ended with three people killed and 20 wounded after the troops of the garrison were called out. Violent incidents followed in Carbonear, Harbour Grace and Harbour Main—where the returning officer had his house pulled down.

5. St. John's West (federal) in 1949. Conservative William J. Browne defeats Liberal Greg Power by a slim margin, despite Premier Smallwood's attempts to intimidate the voters into supporting Power.

6. The 1962 St. John's West federal election. Richard Cashin defeats William Browne by only 24 votes. A new election is called before the count can be contested.

7. Ferryland, 1975 Provincial election. Although the Conservatives won a clear majority, nine recounts were required. The returns in three of the districts (Ferryland, Bonavista North and Exploits) were challenged because of suspected irregularities which, having been proven, resulted in three by-elections. The result in Ferryland was challenged again and a second by-election called. Charlie Power was elected 16 June 1977.

8. The 1924 Bonavista by-election. Sir William Coaker comes out of retirement to take on Prime Minister Walter S. Monroe. Monroe wins.

9. The 1967 Gander provincial by-election. P.C. Harold Collins wins over former mayor Jack Robertson—the first evidence that the "tide was turning" against Smallwood.

10. St John's West, 1923. Sir Michael Cashin comes out of retirement to take on Sir Richard Squires. Squires manages to hang on to his seat by four votes.

11. The 1840 Conception Bay by-election, James Prendergast vs. Edmund Hanrahan. Prendergast was supported by the merchants, Hanrahan by the church. As this was before the secret ballot, people were faced with supporting the clergy's candidate and losing their credit, or supporting the merchant's man and losing the Sacraments. Damned if you do, damned if you don't. On polling day in Carbonear rioting and strife forced the returning officer to close the polls early. Consequently, no return was issued, and the election was declared null and void.

Marine

Longest serving coastal steamers

1. *Glencoe*, 60 years.
2. *Clyde*, 48 years.
2. *Home*, 48 years.
4. *Kyle*, 46 years.
5. *Argyle*, 41 years.
6. *Taverner*, 34 years.
7. *Invermore*, 33 years.
7. *Prospero*, 33 years.
9. *Northern Ranger*, 30 years (1936-66—a second *Ranger* remains in service, having been launched in 1986).

The Alphabet Fleet

These ships were owned by the Reid-Newfoundland Company and were so called because the name of the vessels followed the alphabet, beginning with the letter 'A.' The first eight were built in Scotland and took the names of things Scottish. They were the *Argyle, Bruce, Clyde, Dundee, Ethie, Fife, Glencoe* and *Home*. Eventually, the fleet was augmented by the *Invermore, Kyle, Lintrose* and *Meigle*. For some reason, there was no "J" in the Fleet.

The Splinter Fleet

These 10 wooden vessels were built at Clarenville between 1944 and 1947 and named for Newfoundland communities. Popularly known as the "Splinter Fleet" because of their wooden construction, they were the *Bonne Bay, Burin, Clarenville, Codroy, Exploits, Ferryland, Glenwood, Placentia, Trepassey* and *Twillingate*.

Bowring's Shakespeare Fleet

In the early 19th century, the Bowring Company (at that time

Benjamin Bowring and Son) began building a huge fleet of vessels. In the latter part of the century the company began naming the vessels after characters in Shakespearean plays. There were the *Benedict, Capulet, Cordelia, Desdemona, Hamlet, Imogene, Jessica, Juliet, Miranda, Oberson, Ophelia, Orlando, Othello, Portia, Prospero, Romeo, Rosalind, Silvia, Stephano, Titania, Trinculo* and *Viola*.

Did you know that actress Rosalind Russell got her name from the Bowring's ship of the same name? Her parents had travelled on the ship on a cruise to St. John's from New York. They enjoyed the trip so much they named their daughter Rosalind.

Ten books written by fishermen

1. *The Log of Captain Bob Bartlett* by Robert Bartlett (1928).
2. *Forty-eight Days Adrift: The Voyage of the Neptune II from Newfoundland to Scotland* by Job Kean Barbour (1932).
3. *Old and Young Ahead* by Abram Kean (1935).
4. *Fifty Two Years at the Labrador Fishery* by Nicholas Smith (1936).
5. *S'posin' I Dies in a Dory* by Victor Butler (1977).
6. *The Little Nord Easter: Reminiscences of a Placentia Bayman* by Victor Butler (1980).
7. *Our Life on Lear's Room, Labrador* by Greta Hussey (1981)—not strictly by a fisher*man*, obviously.
8. *A Lifetime Listening to the Waves: Memories of a Labrador Fisherman* by George Poole (1987).
9. *The Letter That Was Never Read: A History of the Labrador Fishery*, one of several books written by fisherman-trapper-businessman Benjamin W. Powell Sr. of Carbonear, Square Island and Charlottetown.
10. *The Burned Baby's Arm*, a novel by Woody Island fisherman Randy Lieb.

Ten dramatic marine rescues

1. Captain William Jackman at Spotted Island. Probably the most dramatic of all sea rescues took place in 1867 when the schooner *Sea Clipper* ran aground near Spotted Island, Labrador. Seeing the peril the *Sea Clipper*'s passengers and crew, Jackman removed most of his clothes and swam through the rough seas and cold temperatures to reach the vessel. One by one he carried the 27 people back to

shore on his back. It is believed, however, that his daring contributed to a deterioration in Jackman's health and his early death at the age of 39.

2. George, Ann and Tom Harvey at Isle aux Morts. In 1828, the *Despatch* ran aground near Isle aux Morts. With her lifeboats smashed and high winds and rough seas all around, the passengers awaited what appeared to be certain death. George Harvey along with his daughter Ann and son Tom rescued 152 people from the vessel. For her part, 17-year-old Ann became known as the 'Grace Darling' of Newfoundland (after an English heroine who, with her father, rescued people off the coast of Northumberland). In 1838 the Harveys were again involved in a major rescue when they helped save the 25 crewmembers of the *Rankin*.

3. The *Pollux* and *Truxtun* at Chamber's Cove. On 18 February 1942 the American supply ship *Pollux* along with the destroyers *Truxtun* and *Wilkes* ran aground and started to break up near St. Lawrence during a storm. People from St. Lawrence and Lawn rushed to the area of the grounding help get the men to shore. Of the 389 men on board 186 were rescued.

4. The *Ethie* at Martin's Point, St. Barbe. This wreck occurred just north of Bonne Bay, on 10 December 1919. It is one of the best-known in Newfoundland marine history, partly because it involved a coastal boat of the Alphabet Fleet. Rescuers on shore waded out into the water to grasp a buoy and attach it so that a boatswain's chair could be set up to transport the passengers on board the *Ethie* to shore. It was dramatic in itself, but two stories which have been disputed by some historians continue to arise whenever the *Ethie* is mentioned. One concerns a baby who is supposed to have been sent to shore in a mailbag. The other concerns a dog which is purported to have caught the rope from the buoy and brought it to land. The alleged heroism of the dog is supposed to have inspired E.J. Pratt's poem about a heroic Newfoundland, "Carlo"—while the 'mailbag' and 'dog' stories have often been run together, to conjure the vision of a Newfoundland dog bringing a baby to shore in a mailbag. In spite of much investigation in the years since, the two stories cannot be confirmed.

5. Tyson and the *Tigress*. On 30 April 1873, Harvey and Company's sealing steamer *Tigress* was making a trip to the ice when it encountered a group of people trapped on an ice floe near Grady on the Labrador Coast. Led by George Tyson, the 20 people had been part of an American scientific expedition to the Arctic. They had been on the ice since 15 October 1872—six and a half months—

and had drifted 1500 miles from the west coast of Greenland. During a snowstorm they had been separated from their ship, the *Polaris*. The remaining members of the *Polaris*'s crew had been rescued by a Scottish whaler.

6. The Castaway of Fish Rock. The *Huntsman* was a sailing vessel lost during a trip to the ice on 28 April 1872. The ship left Bay Roberts on 5 March with a crew of 62, under the command of Robert Dawe. She had taken half a load of seals and headed for the coast of Labrador when a storm came up. Captain Dawe sought shelter, but the ship ran onto a reef near Cape St. Charles. Forty-three of the crew perished when the ship sank quickly, 18 managed to scramble over the side and onto the ice to be later rescued—by a ship called the *Rescue*. The remaining crewmember, Solomon French, climbed onto the reef (known as the Fish Rock) where he was rescued two days later.

7. The *Snorre*. On 15 September 1907, a Norwegian clipper ship, the *Snorre* ran into a northeast gale and was driven onto the rocks at Canaille Head near Bonavista. When he saw that the ship wasn't that far from shore, one crewman jumped into the water only to be crushed to death. Residents of the area, led by Captain Lewis Little, rushed to help the people on board and managed to get a line out to the ship. The captain tied the rope to the forecastle and then to test it went hand over hand to shore. The other crewmen followed. The *Snorre* was smashed against the rocks with such force that she was broken into small pieces.

8. The Wreck of the *Waterwitch*. On 29 November 1875, during a winter storm, the schooner *Waterwitch*, out of St. John's bound for Brigus, ran aground at a place called Horrid Gulch near Pouch Cove. The crew and passengers all managed to get off the ship onto the rocks, but the worst was ahead. Captain Samuel Spracklin and two of his crew climbed several hundred feet from the shoreline to the top of the cliff and then made their way through the snow to Pouch Cove. Rescuers rushed to the scene to try to save the others, who were clinging to the storm-washed rocks along the shoreline. When they arrived at the top of the cliff Pouch Cove fisherman Alfred Moore volunteered to swing down on a rope and help the people below. Eleven of the 20 people on board were rescued. During that same storm seven people died when the *Hopewell* sank at nearby Biscayan Cove.

9. Philip Keough and the *Octavia*. This barquentine, under the command of a Captain Disney, was shipwrecked near Ferryland on 6 August 1883. None of the crew was lost, thanks to the heroic actions

of lightkeeper Philip Keough of Ferryland.
10. The ordeal of the *Lady Hobart*. In 1802 the ship *Lady Hobart* was sunk after being holed by ice well off the coast of Newfoundland. The crew and passengers managed to get off the ship and onto the ice, where the 29 people were rescued by the crew of a schooner out of Lower Island Cove.

Honourable mention, for unique use of a personal flotation device—In 1885 the Trinity to Trinity East ferry capsized, spilling its occupants into the water. The ferryman drowned but two female passengers managed to stay afloat until rescued. They had been buoyed up by air which was trapped under their skirts. One of the women was carrying a baby, Thomas J. Fowlow, who slept through the incident.

Graveyards of the Atlantic

Although St. Shotts is perhaps mentioned most frequently as being "The Graveyard of the Atlantic" there are a number of other locations around the Province which have seen dozens of shipwrecks, many of which resulted in loss of life. Here's a list of some of the more prominent:

1. Belle Isle (the "Isle of Demons").
2. Cape Race.
3. Cape John Gull Island.
4. Cat Harbour, Straight Shore.
5. Green Island, Catalina.
6. The Horse Island Shoals.
7. Baccalieu Island.
8. The Wadhams.
9. Mistaken Point, Trepassey.
10. The Lamaline Ledges.

Arts and Letters

Milestones in Newfoundland theatrical history

Thanks to Denyse Lynde of MUN's English Department for supplying most of this information. I've included a couple of my own as well.

1816. Nicholas Rowe's tragedy "The Fair Penitent" was performed by midshipmen and officers of the Royal Navy, becoming the first full-length play performed in Newfoundland. (In his book *The Oldest City*, Paul O'Neill has the date as 18 March 1817).

1817. Theatre St. John's is formed and stages the first theatrical season in Newfoundland. The company's productions of "Point of Honour" and "Bon Ton or High Life Above Stairs" drew such an audience they had to be held over.

1822. The Masonic Order opens the Amateur Theatre in St. John's. The first production was "Castle Spectre" on 17 February 1823.

1841. Jean Davenport (at the age of 14) becomes the first female to appear on stage in Newfoundland. She took the title role in "Richard the Third."

1861. Mummering was outlawed, following the death of a Bay Roberts resident at the hands of mummers. The law is still on the books.

1930. "Journey's End" is produced by the Great War Veteran's Society in St. John's.

1937. Grace Butt founds the St. John's Players. The company's first production ("The Admirable Crichton") was staged in 1938.

1947. A theatre group from England, the Alexandra Players, perform during the winter season at Pitts Memorial Hall in St. John's.

1949. A theatrical history of the St. John's Players published. Entitled "The St. John's Players: the little theatre in Newfoundland," the work is written by P. Lloyd Soper.

1949. In November a commitment is made to compete in Dominion Drama Festival. The first entry from the Province is in the 1952 festival.

1950. The first regional drama festival held under the auspices of the Newfoundland Drama Festival Society. Groups from St. John's, Harbour Grace and Corner Brook take part. Corner Brook wins top honours for a production of "Ten Little Indians."

1951. Two former members of the Alexandra Theatre group, Leslie Yeo and Hilary Vernon, form the London Theatre Company in St. John's. The company performs weekly for the next six seasons. (The first legitimate theatre production I ever saw was London Theatre's production of "Cinderella" with Charles Mardell and Ruth (Perkins) Mardell at the Bishop Feild Auditorium in 1952 or '53).

1956. Formation of the Theatre Arts Club, the first St. John's group set up especially to bring theatre to the Newfoundland outports.
1962. The first Newfoundland High School drama competition is held in Corner Brook.
1967. Two important firsts in Newfoundland theatrical history: the Arts and Culture Centre opens in St. John's; and the all Canadian Dominion Drama Festival is held there. At the building's official opening, the first performance for the Festival is Tom Cahill's adaptation of Harold Horwood's novel "Tomorrow will be Sunday."
1968. The Open Group forms. The Group stages the first productions of most of the plays of Michael Cook.
1972. The Newfoundland Travelling Theatre Company is set up under director Dudley Cox and tours extensively throughout the Province.
1972. Chris Brookes and Lyne Lunde form the Mummer's Troupe.
1973. Codco forms and stages its first production, "Cod on a Stick."
1973. Michael Cook's "Head, Guts, and Soundbone Dance" wins at the Newfoundland Drama Festival and is the first play to be performed on CBC's "Opening Night" series.
1976. "East End Story" by the Mummer's Troupe opens at LSPU Hall.
1978. Rising Tide Theatre is founded by Donna Butt and David Ross.
1979. The Provincial Drama Academy is formed by Maxim Mazumdar.
1982. Opening of the Stephenville Festival of the Arts.
1993. The Trinity Pageant is created by Rising Tide Theatre. Each summer since, the troupe has mounted the pageant at Trinity.

Fifteen Significant Newfoundland Plays

1. Grace Butt: *The Road Through Melton* (1945).
2. Tom Cahill: *As Loved Our Fathers.*
3. Michael Cook: *The Head, Guts and Soundbone Dance.*
4. Al Pittman: *A Rope Against the Sun.*
5. Codco: *Cod on a Stick.*
6. The Mummers Troupe: *Gros Mourn.*
7. Codco: *The Tale Ends.*
8. Ray Guy: *Young Triffie's Been Made Away With.*
9. The Mummers Troupe: *They Club Seals Don't They?.*
10. Des Walsh: *Tomorrow Will Be Sunday.*
11. Pete Soucy: *Flux.*

12. Janis Spence: *Catlover.*
13. Berni Stapleton: *Woman in a Monkey Case.*
14. Liz Pickard: *Alienation of Lizzie Dyke.*
15. Andy Jones: *Out of the Bin.*

Denyse Lynde's list of influential actors/facilitators

1. Charles Hutton - considered by many to have been our greatest impresario and musician.
2. Johnny Burke - One of our greatest entertainment personalities, Burke was a songwriter, balladeer, actor and playwright.
3. Grace Butt - Playwright, founder of the St. John's Players, actor, teacher and director.
4. Hal Holbrook - yes, THE Hal Holbrook. He was a member of the St. John's Players while he was stationed with the American Forces in Newfoundland.
5. P. Lloyd Soper - Probably best known as a judge, Soper authored a book on the history of the St. John's Players and was a leader in the arts community in Corner Brook. He received an honourary doctorate at the opening of Sir Wilfred Grenfell College in Corner Brook in 1988.
6. Neala Griffen - Founding member of the Northcliffe Drama Club of Grand Falls. As director of the company she won seven consecutive times at the Newfoundland Drama Festival.
7. Sylvia Wigh - Promoter of Amateur theatre, directed St. John's Freelance Players for 30 years, and was a pioneer in radio drama.
8. Maxim Mazumdar - Founder of the Stephenville Festival.
9. Andy Jones - Actor, author and comedian.
10. Mary Walsh, Tommy Sexton, Greg Malone and Cathy Jones of Codco.
11. Chris Brookes - Actor, writer, producer and founder of the Mummer's Troupe.
12. Rick Boland - Actor.
13. Donna Butt - Actor, director and co-founder of Rising Tide Theatre.
14. Denys Ferry - Actor.
15. John Moyse - Actor.
16. Gordon Pinsent - Writer, actor and director. Arguably the most successful of all Newfoundlanders who moved to the mainland.
17. Robert Joy - One of the few Newfoundland actors to be successful in the United States, he's appeared in several major films.

18. David Ferry - Another actor who has been successful outside the Province.

Six major-release movies made in Newfoundland (and one that may have been)

1. *49th Parallel*: A fine war drama from 1941 which picked up an Academy Award and starred Laurence Olivier and James Mason. Much of this film was shot in the Bay of Islands.
2. *Captains Courageous*: Some of the scenes for this 1937 Academy Award-winning Spencer Tracy classic were shot around Port aux Basques.
3. *Orca*: Starring Richard Harris, Richard Widmark and Bo Derek, this 1977 release was largely shot in Petty Harbour.
4. *A Whale for the Killing*: A made-for-TV movie, starring Peter Strauss, this flick was based on Farley Mowatt's book about an incident involving a trapped whale in Burgeo in 1967. The movie was shot in Petty Harbour and Quidi Vidi and aired in 1980. (I'm cheating a little on these next three).
5. *No Highway in the Sky*: Although some of this James Stewart/Jack Hawkins 1951 movie took place in Gander, only a couple of scenes were actually shot there. The rest were done on a sound stage.
6. *Spirit of St. Louis*: Again Jimmy Stewart, this time as aviation pioneer Charles Lindbergh, in a 1957 movie adaptation of Lindbergh's solo flight across the Atlantic. One scene has the plane used in the movie flying out through the Narrows.
7. *Commandos Strike at Dawn*: Starring Paul Muni, this 1942 movie about the Norwegian resistance during World War II was, according to some, shot on Newfoundland's West Coast. Other sources indicate it was shot on the West Coast of Canada. In spite of much searching I have not been able to pin down the location. At this writing it is one of those oft-repeated feature movies on A&E.

Great minds think alike: early Newfoundland trivia books

Long before 'The Original Trivia Show, and long before *Art Rockwood's Newfoundland and Labrador Trivia,* there were the likes of Harris Mosdell and James Murphy. Here are some early Newfoundland trivia books, long since out of print, which you may be able to find in a library or dusty attic.

1. *A Catechism of the History of Newfoundland from the Earliest Accounts to the Close of the Year 1834.* Written as a school text by Harbour Grace newspaperman William Charles St. John, the *Catechism* reduced Newfoundland history and geography to a question-and-answer format. Quite possibly the first book to have been published in Newfoundland.
2. *Notable Events in the History of Newfoundland: Six Thousand Dates of Historical and Social Happenings.* Compiled and published by Maurice Devine and M.J. O'Mara of the *Trade Review* (1900).
3. *England's Oldest Possession: The Colony of Newfoundland; A Useful Compilation of Events in Her History, Valuable to the Native Born and of Much Interest to the Dwellers of Other Climes Who May Visit Her Shores.* By James Murphy. One of a great many trivia-style publications of the Carbonear-born balladeer/folklorist, chosen to carry the banner for the rest of Murphy's pamphlets on the subject because of its catchy title. See below for a selection of Murphy's other trivia compilations.
4. *When Was That?: A Chronological Dictionary of Important Events in Newfoundland Down to and Including the Year 1922.* Compiled by physician, politician and journalist Harris M. Mosdell.
5. *5000 Facts About Newfoundland* by H.M. Mosdell (1923?).
6. *Ye Old St. John's* by Patrick K. Devine. A fascinating and informative anecdotal compilation of "townie trivia" (1935).
7. *Strange Facts About Newfoundland* by Ron Pumphery and Leo E.F. English (195?).

Honourable mention: *Newfoundlandia: a cultural experience.* A game, created by Cliff Brown, which can claim a large share of the credit for the renewed interest in Newfoundland trivia.

The ultimate Newfoundland and Labrador trivia book is, of course, *The Encyclopedia of Newfoundland and Labrador.* Every time I pick it up and read a few pages I find another trivia gem. Unfortunately, the five-volume *Encyclopedia* fails to meet the recognized criteria for a trivia book. They literally do not measure up... being a good bit too large for the flushbox.

As consolation, however, the *Lifetime Achievement Award* for Newfoundland and Labrador trivia goes to Joseph R. Smallwood. All six volumes of the *Book of Newfoundland*, along with almost everything Smallwood himself has written, are jampacked with information of interest to spermologists (that is, trivia collectors). Granted, some Smallwood tomes show *slig..* bias and may be open to question as history, but his twin passions for keeping lists and Newfoundland history are evident in all the many publications he had a hand in. (I include some of Smallwood's personal lists later on.)

James Murphy's pursuits

Smallwood's only real competition for the lifetime award is James Murphy. James Murphy was born in Carbonear in 1868. He became a journalist and was a well known songwriter and balladeer who sometimes collaborated with Johnny Burke. He was also known as the "sealer's poet" and wrote numerous poems about the seal fishery, which is also the subject of his two best-known songs: "The Loss of the Florizel" and "The Southern Cross." In 1895 he compiled and published what may have been the first collection of Newfoundland folk songs called *Songs and Ballads of Terra Nova*. Under the nom-de-plume "Scaliger," James Murphy began to submit poems and songs to the daily newspapers in St. John's. For the most part the verses were attacks on Sir Robert Bond's government. During the 1920s, he wrote and published several little pamphlets that today would fit the 'trivia' genre. The pamphlets included lists of such things as famous people who visited Newfoundland, things tourists should know about Newfoundland, and Newfoundlanders who became famous elsewhere. In addition to *England's Oldest Possession* (see above for the full title) a list of his trivia publications includes:

1. "Customs of the past in Newfoundland."
2. "One hundred things you ought to know about Newfoundland."
3. "Historical events of Newfoundland."
4. "Newfoundland heroes of the sea."
5. "A century of events in Newfoundland."
6. "Newfoundland visited by many renowned persons during past one hundred years."

To give you a flavour of the type of trivia James Murphy was writing, I thought I'd include a condensed version of a few of Murphy's lists. In their original form some of them are quite lengthy.

Murphy's "What Tourists Should Know ...vfoundland" (May 1926)

1. When Newfoundland was discovered: June 24, 1497 (and according to Murphy, Cabot sighted a headland he called Bona Vista or Happy Sight).
2. The Size of Newfoundland: 10th largest island in the world. One third larger than Ireland and an area of 42,734 square miles.
3. When Colonization took Place: in 1502 Bristol merchants Hugh Elliott and Thomas Ashurst obtained a patent or grant from Henry VII to establish a colony, then never acted on it. Robert Thorne came in 1527 but his expedition was a failure. In 1536, a London Merchant named Hoare attempted to colonize Newfoundland. It failed and ended with a shipwreck and cannibalism. Sir Humphrey Gilbert took formal possession in 1583. Then John Guy established a colony in 1610.
4. Newfoundland's population: the 1921 census indicated the population of Newfoundland was 259,259 with Labrador at 3774.
5. Newfoundland's Capital: St. John's, the 1921 census showed 36,424 inhabitants.
6. What we possess: the finest fisheries in the world, we have forests of the finest spruce and pine, and we have lots of minerals.
7. What we exported: for the year ending 30 June 1924—Fisheries - $10,867,496; Agriculture - $12,194; Manufacturers - $5,965,625.
8. About our climate: "Much misconception has existed as to Newfoundland's climate. From June to October it leaves little to be desired. The days are pleasant, and not too hot, and the nights are cool and refreshing, while the weather is settled and more reliable than is the rule in England or the United States."
9. The Newfoundland people: quoting Right Rev. Dr. Mullock "Its people has sprung from the most energetic nations of modern times, English, Irish and Scotch."

Murphy's list of Newfoundlanders who held and who hold high positions in other lands

Murphy originally listed 65 such people. Here are ten of them. This particular subject was also a life-long fascination of Joseph R. Smallwood and remains a perennial favourite on the Trivia show.

1. Lord Edward Patrick Morris - Born at St. John's, May 8, 1859 Morris was twice elected Prime Minister of Newfoundland. One of the foremost lawyers in his day, he resigned the leadership in 1918, and went to London where he was appointed to the House of Lords, the only Newfoundlander to achieve that status.
2. Governor Ambrose Shea - Born at St. John's, Shea held many high positions in the Government of his native land. In 1885 he was appointed Governor of Newfoundland but the position was withdrawn after opposition from the Prime Minister and Chief Justice of Newfoundland. As a consolation Shea was given Governorship of the Bahamas. He retired to England in 1894 and died at London in 1905 at the age of 90 years.
3. Sir Henry Pynn - Born at Mosquito, (now Bristol's Hope) Pynn served as Lieutenant-Colonel in the English and Portuguese Service. Pynn fought in the Napoleonic Wars at Waterloo, and was the first native born Newfoundlander to be knighted. He died at London, England, in 1855.
4. Sir Thomas Roddick - Born at Harbour Grace, Roddick became an eminent Canadian physician, was appointed dean of medicine at McGill University and served as a member of Parliament for eight years. He died at Montreal in 1923.
5. Mayor John Shea - Born at St. John's, Shea was founder of the *Newfoundlander* a well known newspaper of the mid 19th century. In the late 1830s he left Newfoundland and settled down in Cork, Ireland. He married there and in December, 1849 was elected Mayor of Cork, was Honourary Secretary of the National Exhibition held there in 1852, and died in 1858.
6. Lieut-Col. John Hutchings - Born at St. John's, Hutchings spent 33 years in India in the British Army. He commanded the 33rd Regiment and died in 1878 at Haniton, Devon, England, aged 74 years.
7. George Brine - Born at St. John's, Brine left Newfoundland for America while still a youth. He eventually became a Director of the Chicago Board of Trade.
8. John McGrath - McGrath moved to Boston, Massachusetts where he became President of the Boston Interstate Fish Corporation Co. and also Secretary to President Theodore Roosevelt.
9. Capt. Aubrey Crocker - Born at Trinity, Crocker commanded the American yacht *Puritan* which defeated the English yacht *Genesta* in the famous races of 1885. The *Puritan* won the challenge cup on that historic occasion.
10. Capt. Corbin - Born at St. John's, Corbin commanded the 63rd Halifax Rifles, was in the North West Rebellion, won the Governor

General's prize of $250, and a special badge for "target shooting" in Canada in the 1880s.

Smallwood's Lists

J.R. Smallwood was probably Newfoundland's biggest listmaker and trivia nut (and I mean that in the kindest sense). He made lists of everything imaginable. Read any of his books and you'll find lists of all manner of things, from people he met, to dreams unfulfilled, to his family tree (subcategorized into yet more lists of who gained prominence and who lived where, and so on and so on). Whenever he had a new project in mind he started more lists. Here are a few of them.

Joey's prerequisites for the job of Premier of Newfoundland and Labrador

1. Prodigious good health.
2. Equally prodigious physical and mental energy.
3. A personal knowledge of Newfoundland's history and geography.
4. An intimate knowledge of governmental and departmental affairs— such as any smart, interested newspaperman can acquire.
5. Vaulting ambition for Newfoundland.

Smallwood's own assessment of his personal qualifications for the job of Premier

1. I had organized one cooperative society of cod fishermen and one or two other cooperatives.
2. I had organized half a dozen unions and led one successful strike of seal-hunters
3. I had originated and conducted one of the most popular of all radio programs.
4. I had written half a dozen books, several of which were published.
5. I had been organizer and editor of the biggest literary enterprise in Newfoundland history.
6. I had done some farming on Kenmount Road.
7. I had run one of the largest hog-raising establishments in Canada.

Smallwood's two indispensable qualifications for future premiers of Newfoundland

1. They should have served an apprenticeship at cleaning out after pigs (a knowledge of pigs, two-legged as well as four, would be very valuable).
2. They should have spent many hours out on our Newfoundland barrens and marshes, picking berries.

Five admitted failures

A selection of the 23 listed in the chapter "Dreams that Didn't Come True" in J.R. Smallwood's *I Chose Canada*.

1. Failure to duplicate in Newfoundland the little town of Rothenberg in Germany. Smallwood wanted to people his new town with Germans, who would operate the hotels, restaurants, etc. and attract thousands of German tourists. As a followup he considered duplicating towns in Italy and Spain.
2. Failure to line the first 26 miles of the TCH eastward from Port aux Basques with flowering trees and shrubs that would come to blossom in succession throughout a period of several months each year. It would be billed as "the longest lovers' lane in the world."
3. Failure to build in some deserted cove in Newfoundland a perfect replica of a 16th or 17th century fishing village to serve as a tourist attraction.
4. Failure to institute a really powerful policy of conservation and of promotion of our trout and salmon fisheries in Newfoundland and Labrador.
5. Failure to establish a park filled with statues and monuments in front of the Confederation Building—sort of a Newfoundland and Labrador "Hall of Fame." (Joey had hoped to have about 20 including Squantum, the Indian who had lived in Newfoundland for a time and who had become a saviour to the Pilgrims in the U.S. Smallwood only saw 3 completed: Corte Real, Cabot, and Sir Wilfred Grenfell).

J.R. Smallwood's list of the most interesting Newfoundlanders of the 20th Century

1. Sir Robert Bond (Prime Minister).
2. Sir Edward (Lord) Morris (Prime Minister).
3. Sir Richard Squires (Prime Minister).

4. Sir William Coaker (politician, union organizer).
5. Dr. Arthur Barnes (politician, educator and Colonial Secretary under Richard Squires).
6. Sir John Crosbie (businessman, politician and the grandfather of *our* John Crosbie).
7. Sir Michael Cashin (politician, Prime Minister for 6 months in 1919).
8. Sir John Bennett (businessman, politician).
9. Sir Patrick McGrath (journalist, politician, and one of Newfoundland's guiding forces in the Labrador Boundary dispute settlement).
10. Sir Alfred B. Morine (politician, journalist).
11. John Murray Anderson (the music impresario who made his mark in the United States as one of the most influential theatrical producers).
12. Captain Bob Bartlett (mariner renowned worldwide for his exploits).

Obviously, this list is skewed towards politicians: only Bartlett and Anderson were not political figures... and there is one obvious (and uncharacteristically modest) omission. Of the politicians, only Arthur Barnes was not knighted. There were no women listed.

J.R. Smallwood's list of great Newfoundland books

These were listed in his foreword to *Joseph Banks in Newfoundland and Labrador, 1766* by Dr. Averil M. Lysaght, published by University of California Press. Smallwood added Lysaght's book to his choice of the greatest books written about Newfoundland or connected with Newfoundland.

1. Richard Whitbourne. *A Discourse Containing a Loving Invitation ... to all Adventurers ... for the Advancement of His Majesties Most Hopefull Plantation in the New-Found-Lande* (1622).
2. Three books by Sir William Vaughan. Smallwood didn't name them, but we can assume that *The Golden Fleece* and *The Newlander's Cure* are included.
3. W.E. Cormack. *Account of a Journey Across the Island of Newfoundland* (1828).
4. Philip Henry Gosse. One can only assume Smallwood is referring to Gosse's "Entomologia Terrae Novae," a scientific treatise on

Newfoundland insects (unpublished, the manuscript compiled during the mid-1830s is in the National Museums of Canada Library in Ottawa).
5. Daniel Woodley Prowse. *A History of Newfoundland* (1895).
6. George Cartwright. *A Journal of Transactions and Events During a Residence of Nearly Sixteen Years on the Coast of Labrador* (1792).
7. Harold A. Innis. *The Cod Fisheries: the History of an International Economy* (1940).
8. Ralph Greenlee Lounsbury. *The British Fishery in Newfoundland, 1634-1763* (1934).
9. James P. Howley. *The Beothucks or Red Indians* (1915).
10. Vaïnö Tanner. *Outlines of the Geography, Life and Customs of Newfoundland-Labrador* (1944).

Although most of the above are quite familiar to Newfoundlanders interested in the history of the Province, the last item is perhaps less well-known outside Labrador. Tanner, a Finnish geographer, made two expeditions to Labrador in the late 1930s. In addition to the geographic, geological and botanic studies in the *Outlines*, there is also a good deal of information about the people of Labrador, and many photographs.

Bob Cuff's essential Newfoundlandia

I have never met anyone more widely read or versed in Newfoundland and its trivia than Bob Cuff—my publisher, but also for five years managing editor of the *Encyclopedia of Newfoundland and Labrador*. When I set about doing a Book of Newfoundland and Labrador Lists he had lots and lots of suggestions, including this list of books and periodicals that anyone wanting to add to their knowledge of Newfoundland should have in their library. For the uninitiated, however, the best introduction to Newfoundland literature is Patrick O'Flaherty's *The Rock Observed* (1979), even if it is now out of date.
1. George Story, W.J. Kirwin, and J.D.A. Widdowson. *The Dictionary of Newfoundland English* (1982).
2. Daniel Woodley Prowse. *A History of Newfoundland from the English, Colonial and Foreign Records* (1895).
3. *The Encyclopedia of Newfoundland and Labrador* (five volumes).

4. Gerald S. Doyle. *Old Time Songs and Poetry of Newfoundland* (various editions, since 1927).
5. James P. Howley. *The Beothucks or Red Indians* (1915).
6. *Them Days* magazine.
7. S.J.R. Noel. *Politics in Newfoundland* (1973).
8. E.R. Seary. *Family Names of the Island of Newfoundland* (1977).
9. Philip Tocque. *Newfoundland: As it Was and As it Is in 1877.* (1878).
10. *The Book of Newfoundland* (vols. 1 & 2, 1937).

Honourable mentions (in no particular order):

Ray Guy. *You May Know Them as Sea Urchins Ma'am* (1975).
Dillon Wallace. *The Lure of the Labrador Wild* (1905).
J.B. Jukes. *Excursions in and About Newfoundland During the Years 1839 and 1840* (1842).
Nicholas Smith. *Fifty two Years at the Labrador Fishery* (1936).
Peter Neary. *Newfoundland in the North Atlantic World 1929-1949* (1988).
W.A. Munn. *Wineland Voyages* (1914).
Edward Wix. *Six Months of a Newfoundland Missionary's Journal from February to August 1835* (1836).
Richard Whitbourne. *A Discourse Containing a Loving Invitation ... to all Adventurers ... for the Advancement of His Majesties Most Hopefull Plantation in the New-Found-Lande* (1622).
Cassie Brown. *Death on the Ice* (1972).
W.E. Cormack. *Narrative of Journey Across the Island of Newfoundland in 1822* (1828).

People

Nine American show business personalities who served in Newfoundland with the U.S. Forces

1. Actor Hal Holbrook (who performed with the St. John's Players and married a Newfoundland woman).
2-5. The pop Singing group the Four Aces. (One of the group, Dave Mahoney, married Elizabeth Cantwell of St. John's).

6. Actor Victor Mature.
7. Singer Steve Lawrence.
8. Comedian Bill Cosby.
9. Composer-Conductor John Williams.

Ten American show business personalities who appeared in Newfoundland during World War II

1. Actress/singer Joan Blondell.
2. Singer Frank Sinatra.
3. Bandleader Charlie Barnett.
4. Comedian Phil Silvers.
5. Comedian/ventriloquist Edgar Bergen.
6. Comedian Jimmy Durante.
7. Comedian Bob Hope.
8. Actor Andy Devine.
9. Singer Rosemary Clooney.
10. Singer/actress Marlene Dietrich.

Ten great seafaring families

1. Bartletts of Brigus
2. Keans of Flowers Island/Brookfield
3. Winsors of Swains Island/Wesleyville
4. Barbours of Cobblers Island/Newtown
5. Mundens of Brigus
6. Harrises of Grand Bank
7. Burkes of St. Jacques
8. Skinners of Boxey
9. Taylors of Carbonear
10. Dawes of Bay Roberts

Come From Aways—"Mainland" division

People born in other provinces who have made a significant contribution to Newfoundland and Labrador:

Nova Scotia—politician A.B. Morine, Corner Brook mill owner Christopher Fisher, industrialist James Angel and labour leader Earle McCurdy.

New Brunswick—businessman Hazen Russell and nurse Mina (Gilchrist) Paddon.
Prince Edward Island—Prime Minister Philip F. Little and businessman David Smallwood (the grandfather of JRS).
Quebec—Rev. Alexis Belanger, Cartwright businessman S.B. Fequet, railwayman Ferdinand Rioux and suffragist and community activist Armine Nutting Gosling.
Ontario—author Norman Duncan, Grenfell Medical Dr. Gordon Thomas, artist Don Wright, businessman Angus Bruneau and politician and writer Peter Fenwick.
Manitoba—musician Dave Panting, politician J.W. Pickersgill and scientist David Idler.
Saskatchewan—photographer Lorne Rostotski, anthropologist Elliott Leyton and folksinger Omar Blondahl.
British Columbia—historian David Alexander and publisher Ivan Jesperson.

Come From Aways—American division

People from the United States who have made a significant contribution to Newfoundland and Labrador:

Alaska—sportsfisherman Lee Wulff.
Arizona—musician and music educator Leo Sandoval.
Connecticut—Pentecostal Assemblies founder Alice Belle Garrigus.
Illinois—John Shaheen and John C. Doyle (an interesting coincidence, that).
Maryland—"Professor" Charles Danielle.
Massachusetts—novelist R.T.S. Lowell, cod trap inventor W.H. Whiteley, bird behaviourist Bill Montevechhi and MUN administrator Monnie Mansfield.
Michigan—geologist John McKillop.
New Jersey—hard bread baker Robert Vail, marine biologist Fred Aldrich and author Elliot Merrick.
New York—folklorist Herbert Halpert, archaeologist James Tuck and co-op organizer Mary Arnold.
Pennsylvania—jazz musician Ralph Walker.
Rhode Island—*Dictionary of Newfoundland English* co-author, Professor William Kirwin.
South Dakota—broadcaster Bob Lewis (Clarence Engelbrecht) and whale researcher Jon Lien.

Come From Aways—International division

People born elsewhere in the world who have made a significant contribution to Newfoundland and Labrador:

Australia—railwaymen William D. Reid and Harry D. Reid.

Bermuda—businessmen Augustus Harvey, Sir Joseph Outerbridge and William G. Gosling; Chief Justice (and author of "The Banks of Newfoundland") Francis Forbes.

China—businessmen Kim Lee and Davey Fong.

Denmark—Moravian missionary Jens Haven, community activist Jessie Ehlers and photographer Ben Hansen.

Germany—Judge Abe Schwartz, mining promoter Francis von Ellenhausen, religious studies scholar Hans Rollmann and missionary Theodor Bourquin.

Gibraltar—Reverend Ulricus Zwinglius Rule.

Greece—confectioner Christos Giannou.

India—biochemist Thakor Patel and Stephenville drama festival founder Maxim Mazumdar.

Italy—priests Bishop Henry Carfagnini and Diomede Falconio.

Korea—physicist C.W. Cho and Brookfield medical doctor Yong Kee Jeon.

Latvia—businessman Ernest Leja.

Lebanon—businessman Kaleem Noah.

Netherlands—landscape architect Rudolf Cochius and sculptor Hans Melis.

Northern Ireland—journalist/writer Reverend Moses Harvey and businessman James MacBraire.

Norway—businessman Olaf Olsen, pioneer settler Torsten Andersen and fisheries scientist Adolf Neilsen.

Pakistan—physicist Mohammed Irfan.

Phillipines—Twillingate medical doctor Robert Garcia.

Poland—businesswoman/community activist Esther Wilansky and Moravian missionary Benjamin Kohlmeister.

Russia—businessman Israel Perlin.

Scotland—railway contractor R.G. Reid, patriot/medical doctor William Carson, Prime Minister Sir Robert Thorburn and geologist Alexander Murray.

Syria—photographer/businessman Anthony Tooton.

Wales—Reverend John Jones and Reverend Oliver Jackson.

Ten Newfoundlanders who overcame their handicaps

1. Businessman Max Simms (crippled by diabetes).
2. Businessman Clayton King (legs lost in the Viking disaster).
3. Businesswoman Esther Wilansky (blindness).
4. Athlete Mel Fitzgerald (polio).
5. Athlete Joanne Macdonald (spina bifida).
6. St. John's municipal councillor Marie White (paraplegic).
7. Politician A.W. Piccott (loss of a hand).
8. Educator Lowell Legge (blindness).
9. Musician Terry Kelly (blindness).
10. King's Cove watchmaker Kenneth Monk (crippled by an accident).

Most common family names of the Island of Newfoundland (compiled by E. R. Seary)

1. White
2. Parsons
3. Smith
4. Power
5. Walsh
6. King
7. Murphy
8. Brown
9. Ryan
10. Young

Many Whites and Youngs on the West Coast of the Island trace their origins to the French family names LeBlanc and Lejeunne.

Most common family names of Labrador (compiled from the 1995 telephone directory and voter's lists)

1. Anderson/Andersen
2. Rumbolt/Rumbold
3. Penney
4. Brown
5. Russell
6. Michelin
7. White
8. Blake
9. Saunders
10. Williams

Beothuk Indians who lived for a time in white society

1. The 57 Beothuk captured by the Portuguese explorer Corte Real in 1501.

2. John August, who fished at Trinity and Catalina (died at Trinity, 29 Oct. 1788).
3. Oubee, a young girl captured at Charles Brook in 1791. She went to England with Thomas Stone of Trinity in 1792 and died there a few years later.
4. Tom June, who lived at Fogo 1760-95.
5. Demasduit (Mary March) captured by John Peyton Jr. at Red Indian Lake in 1819, died at Ship Cove (Botwood) in 1820.
6. Shawnawdithit (Nancy April) captured with her mother and sister at Badger Bay in 1823 by furrier William Cull. Her mother and sister died at Exploits, Shawnawdithit at St. John's in 1829.

Women in the Newfoundland public service in 1852

1. Eliza Solomon (3rd clerk, St John's Post Office). Her brother, William Solomon, became postmaster general that year.
2. Ann Cross (part-time postmistress at Trinity).
3. Mary Morris (part-time postmistress at Placentia)

Influential Newfoundland and Labrador women

My thanks to Linda Kealey of MUN's History Department for passing along her choices

1. Shanawdithit (Nancy April). This Beothuk woman died in 1829. Her significance lies in passing on to us so much of what we know about Beothuk lore.
2. Frances Knowling (Fannie) McNeil (1869-1928). The most important leader of the suffrage movement after World War I.
3. Julia Salter Earle (1878-1945). Another suffragist, Salter Earle was also an important organizer of working women during World War I and after as head of the ladies Branch of the Newfoundland Industrial Workers Association.
4. Mary Southcott (1862-1943). Established the first training school for nurses at the General Hospital, where she was the first nursing superintendent. Active in a number of causes, including the Child Welfare Association.
5. Vera Perlin (1902-1974). Founder of the Home and School Association, she was also known for her work with handicapped children. The Vera Perlin School was named in her honour.
6. Ella Manuel (1902-1984). Author and a founder of Brownies in Newfoundland.

7. Grace Sparkes (1908-). Journalist, educator and politician.
8. Nancy Riche (1944-). Labour movement activist, at this writing a vice-president of the Canadian Labour Congress.
9. Mary West Pratt (1935-). Artist.
10. Mary Walsh and Cathy Jones. Two of our best known performers. Through Codco, "This Hour has 22 minutes" and other projects frequent collaborators in bringing a taste of Newfoundland to national audiences.
11. Bernice Morgan. Author of *Random Passage* and *Waiting for Time*, arguably the two best novels to have been written about life in Newfoundland.
12. Elizabeth Goudie, Lydia Campbell and Millicent Blake Loder. Three who have brought the life of Labrador women to others through their autobiographies.
13. Lady Constance M. Harris (?-1941). Directed the Women's Patriotic Association and launched an Outport Nursing Scheme in 1920 recruiting midwives from England to serve in Newfoundland outports. (Others, including Lady Elsie Allardyce also made significant contributions to the nursing scheme and NONIA in the early 1920s.)

Places

The most common place/feature name in Newfoundland and Labrador (according to the 1983 *Gazetteer*), is Long Pond, of which there are 87—Long is also the most common name for a Point (56), and is among the commonest names of an Island (19).

Familiar coves

The most common name for a cove is Wild Cove (31 occurrences). There are more than 20 coves on the Island with each of the following names:

1. Wild Cove.
2. Back Cove.
3. Broad Cove.
4. Seal Cove.
5. Caplin Cove.
6. Bear Cove.
7. Green Cove.
8. Shoal Cove.
9. Ship Cove.
10. Herring Cove.

The most common names for an island

1. Green Island (56).
2. Gull Island (46).
3. Pigeon Island (42).
4. Duck Island (36).
5. Flat Island (25).
6. Red Island (23).
7. Burnt Island (20).
8. Black Island (19).
9. Long Island (19).
10. Big Island (18).

The most common names for a pond

1. Long Pond (87).
2. Gull Pond (59).
3. Rocky Pond (57).
4. Island Pond (54).
5. Beaver Pond (44).
6. Round Pond (30).
7. Second Pond (30).

There are many more Second Ponds than First Ponds (19). Incidentally, there are 21 Third Ponds, 11 Fourths, three Fifths and two Sixth Ponds.

Other points of interest

1. Long Point (56).
2. White Point (47).
3. Shoal Point (32).
4. Green Point (23).

The most common name for a rock is Black (44, as opposed to 22 White Rocks).

The most common name for a brook is Rattling Brook (21). There also 21 places called The Narrows.

Newfoundland having been purportedly discovered on Saint John the Baptist's feast day (24 June), it is perhaps not surprising that the saint most commonly invoked in placenames is John (28 occurrences). Newfoundland also has several places named after saints on the old French Shore, which retain a Breton spelling, or are of saints important in the Breton liturgical year (Barbe, Lunaire, Modeste).

There are even places named after made-up saints, thought to be poorly-conceived attempts to anglicize a placename: St. Shott is not to be found in any histories of the christian church.

Most unusual placenames (abandoned communities)

1. Roundabout (Burin Peninsula).
2. Drook (near Cape Race).
3. Pushthrough (South Coast).
4. Zealot (French Shore).
5. Venom's Bight (Baie Verte Peninsula).
6. Rosiru (Placentia Bay).
7. Mother IXX (St. Mary's Bay). Maybe the problem of how to pronounce IXX led to the community being renamed Regina.
8. St. Jones Without (Trinity Bay).
9. Toslow (Placentia Bay).
10. Quiller and/or Goblin (right across Bay D'Espoir from each other).

A now-abandoned community in St. Mary's Bay once revelled in the name Pinchgut Tickles. An attempt by a well-meaning priest to change the name to Assumption Passage was abandoned after it was found that locals invariably spoke of it as Consumption Passage, and the shortened name "Tickles" was adopted instead.

Unusual placenames (current communities)

1. Come by Chance.
2. Seldom Come By.
3. Kitchuses.
4. Boswarlos.
5. Too Good Arm.
6. Dildo.
7. Herring Neck.
8. Nameless Cove.
9. Happy Adventure.
10. Spread Eagle.
11. Joe Batt's Arm.

Honourable mention: The Pond That Feeds the Brook (near North River, Conception Bay).

Most unusual placenames (Labrador division)

1. Run by Guess.
2. Triangle.
3. Scrammy.
4. Sheshatshit.
5. Bobbin Joys.
6. Butter n Snow.
7. Punchbowl.
8. Strawberry.
9. Tumbledown Dick.
10. Domino.

Honourable mention: Fish Cove and Cod Island. Newfoundland is noticeably lacking in placenames that contain "cod" or "fish."

Placenames from Languages other than English or French

Basques: Port aux Choix, Placentia, New Ferolle and Port au Port.
Beothuk: Shannoc (Noel Pauls) Brook and Aguathuna.
Hebrew/Aramic: Hebron and Nain.
Inuktituk: Okak and Saglek (in fact, the majority of placenames north of Cape Harrison).
Innu: Sheshatshit; Menihek and Lake Michikamau (as well as many lakes and rivers in Labrador interior).
Irish Gaelic: Cappahayden, Kilbride, Skibberean and Ballyhack (the last two being neighbourhoods near Holyrood).
Italian: Bonavista.
Micmac: lakes Meelpaeg, Kaegudeck and Medonnegonix.
Norse: Markland.
Portuguese: Baccalieu, Ferryland (from Farilham) and Old Bonaventure.
Scots Gaelic: Lomond and Loch Leven.
Spanish: Carbonear.

Small towns

All these places had populations in single digits in the 1991 census.

1. Lockston (population, 1). Near Trinity, the community has been almost exclusively summer cabins for some years.
2. Red Island, Placentia Bay (1). As with many others on the list, Red Island was resettled in the 1960s and has since been reoccupied.
3. Woody Island, Placentia Bay (1). After being the sole inhabitant for several years, Randy Lieb has married since the census was taken. At this writing he and Elvira have had two children—and were threatening to take Woody Island out of the top ten.
4. Daniel's Cove, Trinity Bay (2). North of Old Perlican.
5. Woods Island, Bay of Islands (3).
6. Newport, Bonavista Bay (3).
7. Charles Brook, Exploits Bay (3).
8. L'Anse au Loup (3). Near Grand Bank.
9. Hodderville, Bonavista Bay (4).
10. Placentia Junction (6).
11. Ship Cove, Placentia Bay (8). Ship Cove is home to the Tobin family's creamery and probably has the largest per-capita butter production of any community in Canada!

Off the beaten track: unheralded Newfoundland beauty spots

In the course of work for the *Encyclopedia of Newfoundland and Labrador*, researchers travelled into all sorts of nooks and crannies. Here is a list of some favourite places, compiled by Bob Cuff.

1. *Greenland* (Burnt Head, Cupids). An abandoned community with a matchless view of Conception Bay.
2. *Burgeo Sandbanks*. Not many people associate the Southwest Coast with trackless sandy beaches—but here they are, just the same. The site of a provincial park.
3. *Round Harbour* (Notre Dame Bay). The road goes to the head of the harbour, but thereafter you're on foot. A gem of a harbour and a true taste of days gone by.
4. *Gaultois Passage*. A narrow, 10-mile long channel between Long Island and the main—northwest of the scenic town of Gaultois. Identified on most maps as "Little Passage."
5. *Englee*. A pretty and historic town—take the walking trail to the old lighthouse for a breathtaking view of Canada Bay.
6. *Main River, Sops Arm*. The river valley is unforgettable, and the arm itself a joy. Sops Arm River Provincial Park is located right on the delta where the two meet.
7. *Newtown* (Bonavista Bay). The town is built on a series of rocky islets and was once known as "the Venice of the Newfoundland." Recently, two fine houses that once belonged to a legendary family of mariners (the Barbours) have been opened to the public. Just to the north, Newtown has its Lido—the sand beaches of Cape Island and Cape Freels.
8. *Stephenville Crossing*. Amazing tidal flats—one of the best places in Newfoundland for bird-watching.
9. *Pool's Cove* (Fortune Bay). One of Newfoundland's prettiest villages.
10. *English Harbour* (Trinity Bay). The scenery of Trinity and its outharbours has long been appreciated by Newfoundlanders, but is just starting to get wider recognition. The appeal of English Harbour among all the beauty spots in the area is hard to pin down—but it is there nonetheless.

Our Judiciary and Laws

Sir Humphrey Gilbert's three laws

When Sir Humphrey Gilbert took possession of Newfoundland for the Queen of England on 5 August 1583 he also proclaimed three laws. Sir George Peckham, who accompanied Gilbert on his voyage, wrote that they were:

1. The Religion be publiquely exercised, should be such, and none other, than in the Church of England.
2. If any person should bee lawfully convicted of any practise against her Majestie, her Crowne and dignitie, to be adjudged as traitors according to the Lawes of England.
3. If any should speake dishonourably of her Majestie, the party so offending to loose his eares, his ship and goods to be confiscate to the use of the Generall.

John Guy's Laws

This legal code was devised by John Guy at Cupids to provide order in the colony before his return to England in 1611. They were proclaimed on 30 August 1611, much to the dismay of migrant West Country fishermen (who far out numbered the colonists at this stage in Newfoundland history)—at least until they realized that Guy had no way to carry out the proposed sentences.

1. Ballast or anything hurtful to harbours not to be throwne out but to be carriedd ashore—Penalty 5 pounds for every offence.
2. No person to destroy, deface, or spoile any stage cooke room flakes &c.—Penalty 10 pounds.
3. Every Admiral of each harbour for time being reserve only so much beach and flake or both as is needful for number of boats—Penalty 10 pounds.
4. No person to deface or alter markes of any boates—Penalty 5 pounds.
5. No person to convert to his own use, boates belonging to others

without their consent except in case of necessity and then to give notice to Admiral—Penalty 5 pounds.
6. No person to set fire in woods—Penalty 10 pounds.
7. No person at end of voyage to destroy stage cooke room or flakes that he hath that year used—Penalty 10 pounds.
8. No master of any ship to receive into his ship any person of the Colony, that are already planted by virtue of His Majesty's gracious Patent without speciall warrant under the handwriting of the Governor of the Colony or Colonies in the Newfoundlande aforesaid.

Celebrated legal cases

1. *The Labrador boundary reference.* The determination of the Labrador boundary had been an issue between Newfoundland and Quebec since the 18th century. A Royal Proclamation and the Treaty of Paris of 1763 set the boundary and gave Newfoundland jurisdiction over the coast of Labrador. In the years following Quebec disputed where the actual boundary lines were drawn and who had jurisdiction over what. Subsequently the territory was annexed to Quebec in 1774, then back to Newfoundland in 1809. In 1904 the Canadian Government suggested that Quebec and Newfoundland take their dispute to the Judicial Committee of the Privy Council where it could be settled once and for all. Newfoundland agreed in 1907, but it was not until 21 October 1926 (after both parties had gathered evidence to support their claims) that they appeared before the Privy Council. In the intervening years Newfoundland offered to sell its control over Labrador to Quebec but the offer was turned down. The main problem facing the Judicial Committee was a definition of the word "coast" and determining what really constituted a coast. Some 5000 pages of evidence had been gathered by Sir Patrick T. McGrath to support Newfoundland's claim. On 1 March 1927 the council handed down its judgement reaffirming Newfoundland's jurisdiction over Labrador. Ironically a few years later Newfoundland again offered to sell Labrador to Quebec or Canada, this time for 100 million dollars. It was during the depression and the offer was turned down.
2. *The Chinese murders.* On 3 May 1922 Wo Fen Game, a Chinese immigrant worker in St. John's, shot three Chinese co-workers to death, wounded his brother-in-law, and tried to commit suicide. He was charged with murder, in what was probably the most widely followed trial in Newfoundland to that time. During the trial it was learned that the accused was dissatisfied with what he was being paid in the laundry where he worked and felt his co-workers planned to kill him. After an

eventful trial Wo Fen Game was found guilty and sentenced to death. He was hanged on 16 December 1922.

3. *The flogging of Butler and Landrigan.* In the early nineteenth century it was not unusual for people to receive severe punishment for the simplest of wrongdoings. Court was often conducted by naval officers as "surrogate" judges, many of whom were probably used to meting out quarter-deck justice, and who had little understanding of the complexities of the law. In 1818 James Landrigan (or Lundrigan) of Cupids was charged for a debt of 12 pounds. Landrigan eventually was brought before Captain David Buchan and the Rev. John Leigh (then the Anglican parish priest at Harbour Grace), found guilty and sentenced to receive 36 lashes for his misdeeds. In addition to the matter of his debts, Landrigan had failed to show up for court on the day appointed, and this didn't sit well with Buchan, who considered it to be high contempt. Landrigan was also to have his property confiscated. The physical punishment was so severe that Landrigan fainted after 14 lashes. This incident combined with another involving a man named Butler from Harbour Main so enraged the populace that a number of protests were held. The cause was taken to England where in 1824 the Imperial Parliament passed "An Act for the Better Administration of Justice in Newfoundland."

4. *Kent vs Kielley.* Dr. Edward Kielley was a St. John's physician. In 1838 he became embroiled in a dispute with John Kent, a member of the House of Assembly. Kent had criticized the management of the St. John's Hospital while protected by the privilege of the House. The doctor was outraged and in a public confrontation with Kent accused the member of being a liar and shook his fist in Kent's face. The matter was taken to the Bar of the Assembly and Kielley was called in and charged with having attacked one of the members. Kielley wasn't permitted to speak in his own defence and after accusing Kent of being a liar, was found to be in a breach of House privileges and taken from the House and off to jail. Next day Kielley appeared in court where Judge George Lilly ruled that the House had exceeded its powers and Kielley was released. The Speaker of the House, William Carson, did not appreciate the court's decision and demanded the arrest of Kielley, the Judge and the High Sheriff. The case was heard before the Supreme Court which ruled in Carson and Kent's favour. Kielley appealed to the Privy Council in England. After reviewing the case, the council decided in Dr. Kielley's favour and ruled to limit the authority of colonial legislatures throughout the British Empire.

5. *The jailing of Robert John Parsons by Henry Boulton.* On 11 May 1835 an anonymous letter appeared in the newspaper *Newfoundland Patriot*, commenting on a charge Chief Justice Henry Boulton had made to a jury about the benefits of hanging as a form of punishment. The judge viewed the letter as contempt and called for Robert John Parsons, the paper's editor, to appear before him. Parsons refused to name the author of the letter and told the judge the proceedings were illegal and unconstitutional, as the judge could not act in an impartial manner in the matter before the court. Parson's defence did little to prick Boulton's sense of self-importance. The judge declared that, as the author of the letter was unnamed, the editor of the *Patriot* must assume full responsibility for its publication. He sentenced Parsons to three months in jail and a fine of 50 pounds. The populace of St. John's was outraged. Parsons' supporters paid his fine and within days he was released from jail. Shortly afterwards Boulton was removed from his position and moved to Toronto.

6. *Baird vs Walker.* In 1713 the Treaty of Utrecht set the boundaries of the French Shore from Cape Bonavista along the coast to the tip of the Great Northern Peninsula then South to Point Riche. The Treaty of Versailles revised the boundaries so that they became Cape St. John to the tip of the Northern Peninsula then south to Cape Ray. The ruling gave French fishermen special privileges over the shore even though they could only stay there during the fishing season and any buildings erected had to be for the prosecution of the fishery. There were numerous disputes between English fishermen and the French over the Shore. One of the most serious involved the setting up of lobster factories by Newfoundland, American and Nova Scotian interests. The French saw it as a treaty violation. Attempts to settle the dispute failed and in 1889 a temporary agreement (modus vivendi) was drawn up. The agreement prohibited the operation of any lobster factories not in operation on 1 July 1889 except by joint consent of the French and British senior naval officers. One operation that had been established after the July date was that of James Baird. It was shut down by Admiral Sir Baldwin Walker. Baird challenged the legality of Walker's actions. The Supreme Court agreed with Baird that the admiral had acted outside his jurisdiction and the court decision was upheld by the Privy Council. In effect, the case ended the authority exercised by naval officers along the shore and underlined the importance of deciding the jurisdictional problems along the French Shore.

7. *The Corrupt Practices prosecutions.* In November 1893 Sir Wil-

liam V. Whiteway's Liberals won a general election over the Conservatives. It had been a rough campaign with much name-calling and mud-slinging. In January the following year the Conservatives retaliated. Under a recently-passed piece of legislation known as the Corrupt Practices Act, they brought charges of corruption and bribery against 15 members of the Liberal party and one independent. The Conservatives claimed that the accused had used promises of government work to get votes. All 16 were found guilty by the court and their election declared null and void. On April 11 Whiteway resigned and the Conservative leader Augustus Goodridge was asked by the Governor to form a new administration.

8. *Reid vs Morine.* In 1898, following his election, Conservative Prime Minister James Winter and his Receiver General Alfred Morine set out to negotiate a railway contract with Robert G. Reid. When signed the agreement gave Reid control of the railway for 50 years. It also made Reid the biggest landholder in the world. The Liberal members of the House took the government to task when it was learned that while Morine was negotiating on behalf of the government he was also on a retainer to Reid... a fairly blatant conflict of interest!

Morine resigned his seat. He returned to the House in 1899 after leaving Reid's employ but soon resigned again in a dispute with the Prime Minister. Shortly afterwards, Winter's government fell in a vote of non-confidence and the reins of power went to the Liberals under Robert Bond. In the ensuing election the main issue was re-negotiation of the railway contract. By now, Morine was leading the Conservatives but his reputation of being Reid's lacky hung over him. Bond's Liberals all but annihilated the Conservatives who only picked up two of the 36 seats while the Liberals took 32. Bond's first order of business was to get a fairer deal for Newfoundland from the railway contract.

Although many of the details of the arrangements between Reid and Morine became public during the election campaign of 1900, it was not until 1906 that all the dirty linen was aired—when Reid sued Morine over ownership of the *Daily News*. The court case proved so embarrassing that Reid eventually paid Morine $10,000 a year to stay out of Newfoundland.

9. *The Canning murder.* On 12 May 1899, St. John's saloon owner Francis Canning was hanged for the murder of a barmaid, Mary Nugent. There appeared to be no motive for the killing, except that Canning, who had been described as being a kind man, would become violent after drinking. A statement given by Nugent before

her death indicated she was taking off her coat when she was shot in the back by Canning. At his trial Canning was found guilty. But the people of Newfoundland were by this time largely opposed to the harshness of the death penalty, and wanted to see clemency. Prayers were said on Canning's behalf and a vigil was kept outside the prison—in the worst thunderstorms St. John's had seen in a quarter-century. Following the execution, newspaper columnists commented that they hoped it would be the last execution in Newfoundland. It was not.

10. *The murder of Judge Keen.* William Keen was a highly regarded merchant, who fought for local justice during the early 18th century and was later himself appointed magistrate. In 1754 he was murdered during an attempted robbery at his home. Ten people were brought to trial, one of whom turned King's evidence. At the conclusion of the trial a jury deliberated for only a half hour before returning a guilty verdict against the nine defendants. The judge sentenced them to be hanged, and ordered that the two men who had struck the fatal blows be taken down after death and strung up in chains in a public place. One of the nine people was Eleanor Power, a former servant in Keen's household who had convinced her co-conspirators that a box under his bed contained money and other valuables. Her hanging is believed to have been the first execution of a female in British North America. (Incidentally, during the course of the fatal robbery the miscreants forced Judge Keen's strongbox, to find that it contained only liquor.)

11. *The Trial of Stephen Ratkai.* One of the more unusual trials in our history, this 1989 trial was the first time anyone had been tried in Newfoundland for espionage. Ratkai was born in Nova Scotia and had worked at the U.S. naval base in Argentia. He was arrested and charged with having spied for the Soviet Union. It was said that he had obtained classified documents and turned them over to the Russians. A sting operation by the U.S. Navy caught Ratkai in the act. He was tried and convicted and sentenced to nine years in prison.

Ten celebrated jurists

1. Charles E. Hunt.
2. Sir Brian Dunfield.
3. Clyde K. Wells.
4. Sir James S. Winter.
5. William J. Higgins.
6. D.W. Prowse.
7. Sir William H. Horwood.
8. Harry Winter.
9. Sir Hugh W. Hoyles.
10. Sir Bryan Robinson.

Notable People and Events

Six famous Newfoundland natives

1. Shanawdithit (Nancy April). Last of the Beothuk, she died in June 1829.
2. Demasduit (Mary March). The wife of Nonobawsut, she was captured by John Peyton Jr. in 1819 and died the following year.
3. Nonobawsut. Thought to have been the last of the great Beothuk chiefs, he was killed by Peyton's party after he tried to get his wife away from her captors.
4. Sylvester Joe. A Micmac who accompanied William Cormack on his journey across Newfoundland in 1822.
5. Squantum (or Tisquantum). A member of the Pawtuxet band of the Wampanoag Indians, he was captured and taken to Spain in 1614. He escaped and made his way to England. Squantum came to Newfoundland in 1616, returned to England in 1618 and back to New England the following year. Squantum was instrumental in saving the Pilgrims colonists by showing them how to plant corn and catch fish.
6. Matty Mitchell. A Micmac-Montagnais propector and guide, best known for having discovered the Buchans orebody in 1905.

Shanawdithit's gifts to William E. Cormack

In January 1829 Shanawdithit gave to Cormack a pair of smooth stones used in divination rites by the Beothuks and, after some coaxing, a lock of her hair.

Cormack's gifts to the Royal Scottish Museum in Edinburgh

On 31 October 1827 William Cormack and his Micmac guides left the mouth of the Exploits River to make a trip to the interior of the island. His hope was to find traces of the Beothuks. Instead he found a cemetery in which was buried the remains of Demasduit (Mary March), her husband Nonosabasut and their infant child. Early the next year he travelled to Scotland and made a presentation of the artifacts to the Royal Scottish Museum in Edinburgh.

1. The skull of a male Red Indian.
2. The skull of a female Red Indian.
3. A model of a canoe made by Red Indians.
4. The point of a spear.
5. Two meat dishes and a drinking cup made of bark.
6. Two small wooden figures.
7. Iron pyrites, which had been used as fire stones.

Most of the artifacts have disappeared in the intervening years. The only items remaining are the skulls and the model of the canoe.

Events which happened in Newfoundland that had a significant impact on the world

1. 1497. John Cabot reports fish can be taken in baskets, inspiring European countries to send fishing vessels.
2. 1763. Governor Thomas Graves hires James Cook as surveyor. The survey gave Newfoundland its first accurate maps and launched Captain Cook on a career which saw him recognized as the greatest explorer of the age.
3. 1800. Rev. John Clinch of Trinity vaccinates his nephew and children for smallpox, after Dr. Edward Jenner sent the minister threads of the vaccine. It was the first time a vaccine was used in North America.
4. 1866. The landing of transatlantic telegraph cable. After three previous attempts had failed, on 27 July the ship *Great Eastern* landed a cable at Heart's Content. The completion of the venture was the first direct communications link between North America and Europe.
5. 1901. Guglielmo Marconi receives first transatlantic wireless transmission. On 12 December at Signal Hill Marconi received the letter 'S' transmitted by a station in Poldhu, England, proving that long distance wireless communication was possible.
6. 1912. The *Titanic* sinks after hitting an iceberg about 650 km off Cape Race. Of the 2200 people on board, 1522 perish. After the tragedy a number of recommendations were made to prevent future disasters of this type. Included was the provision of enough lifeboats for all on board, more watertight bulkheads and better lookout.
7. 1919. John Alcock and Arthur Whitten Brown complete the first

non-stop transatlantic airplane flight. Leaving Lester's Field in St. John's on 14 June, they landed on a bog at Clifden, Ireland 16 hours and 57 minutes later after an eventful flight.
8. 1941. The construction of Goose Bay Airport. Recognizing the need to provide an airbase to protect northeastern North America from air attack by Germany, the Canadian Government decided to build the airport on a sandy plateau in Labrador. At first known as Canada Bay, the airport's name was changed to RCAF Station Goose Bay on 1 April 1942. With the arrival of the American forces the airport was expanded so that by June 1943 it was the world's largest airport.
9. 1941. The death of Frederick Banting. A plane carrying the Nobel prize-winning co-discoverer of insulin crashed near Musgrave Harbour, en route to England where Dr. Banting was to aid in the War effort.
10. 1941. The signing of Atlantic Charter near Ship Harbour, Placentia Bay. This was the first meeting of Allied leaders during World War II. U.S. President Franklin D. Roosevelt and British Prime Minister Winston Churchill met for three days on a ship off Argentia and signed an agreement which set out the united aims of the United States and Great Britain.
11. *c*. 1012. Skraelings attack the Vikings, probably near Rigolet. The "skraelings" were a native people who were first encountered by the Norse in about 1005. In an expedition headed by Thorvald, a small group of skraelings were killed by the Norse visitors. The skraelings retaliated and Thorvald himself was killed. In 1009 an expedition under the guidance of Thorfinn Karsefni began friendly relations with the skraelings, but it too failed when disagreements and violence broke out between the two groups at L'anse aux Meadows. Karlsefni returned to Greenland, effectively bringing an end to the first attempt by Europeans to colonize the new world.

Ten Newfoundland contributions to polar exploration

Captain Bob Bartlett is the best-known of Newfoundland's polar explorers, but was not the only one. The following is only a partial list of the Newfoundland ships and men which took part in attempts to conquer the poles, as well as scientific study.

1. 1881-82. Captain Richard Pike of Harbour Grace takes the sealing steamer *Proteus* to Lady Franklin Bay to drop off a scientific expedition headed by American Adolphus W. Greely. A year later Pike returned to pick up Greely's group, but the *Proteus* was lost in the

ice. To reach safety, Pike and his crew crossed 600 miles of ice. The survivors of the Greely party were not rescued until 1884, by the Newfoundland sealers *Bear* and *Thetis*.
2. 1892-93. Captain Pike and the *Kite* and Henry B. Bartlett in the *Falcon* take a Robert Peary expedition to Greenland.
3. 1898-1902. Captain John Bartlett and the *Windward* participate in Peary's first assault on the North Pole. (In 1869, at the age of 21, John Bartlett had carried the American explorer Isaac Hayes to Greenland, beginning the Bartlett family's long association with polar exploration.)
4. 1908-09. Captain Robert Bartlett, who had been first mate under his uncle during the *Windward* expedition, commands the *Roosevelt* on Peary's third polar expedition.
5. 1909. Bowring's *Terra Nova*, which had taken part in an Arctic expedition 1894-97 and the first Robert Falcon Scott expedition to the Antarctic in 1903, was purchased by the British Admiralty for the Scott expedition of 1909 (in which Scott's party achieved the South Pole, only to perish before they could get back to the ship. The *Terra Nova*'s first mate during the expedition, Victor Campbell, and a six-man geological party spent six months in a crude ice cave—but survived. Campbell later retired to Black Duck, near Stephenville.
6. 1913. Bob Bartlett takes the *Karluk* on an ill-fated Canadian expedition to the western Arctic.
7. 1926-38. Captain Bob Bartlett and the *Effie M. Morrissey* make annual voyages to Greenland and Ellesmere Island, assisting in pioneering studies in archaeology, marine life, botany, meteorology and natural history.
8. 1928. Jack Bursey of St. Lunaire joins Admiral Richard E. Byrd's American expedition to the Antarctic as a dogteam driver, later winning the Congressional Medal of Honour for his contributions to the expedition.
9. 1933-36. Sergeant George Makinson serves aboard the *R.C.M. Police St. Roch* in the Canadian Arctic—a vessel best known for having been the first ship to navigate the Northwest Passage. On retiring from the R.C.M.P., Makinson returned to the family farm at Makinsons and served as Member of the House of Assembly for Port de Grave.
10. 1944. Captain Robert C. Sheppard of Harbour Grace takes the *Eagle II* and an all-Newfoundland crew on a mission to re-open British bases in the South Atlantic and Antarctic. Sheppard and his crew return the next year to resupply the bases on the *Trepassey*.

Events elsewhere which had a great effect on Newfoundland

1. *The Napoleonic Wars.* The Napoleonic and French Revolutionary Wars lasted from 1795 to 1815. It was during these wars that a number of factors brought about some of the biggest changes in Newfoundland's history. The fishery shifted from a migratory one to one that was resident-based. The demand for able bodied seamen to fight for Britain in the wars took many men who had been involved in the fishery and pressed them into service. Others, fearful of the press gangs, left Britain for Newfoundland. It was also a time of prosperity in the Newfoundland fishery brought about by restrictions on maritime trade. Napoleon introduced his Continental System which cut off trade between Britain and Europe. The British retaliated by blockading ports supplying Napoleon and the United States got into the fray by imposing their own trade embargo on Great Britain. Ironically one of the spinoffs of this was an increased trade between Newfoundland and the West Indies and southern Europe. The demand for fish was still there. By the end of the Napoleonic Wars, the Newfoundland fishery was enjoying its greatest level of prosperity ever.
2. *The Great Depression.* Newfoundland's economy during the 1930s was largely resource-based, depending on the sales of fish, forest products and minerals. With the arrival of the Great Depression, Newfoundland's export markets all but disappeared. By 1933, the Colony was in such a bad state that the British Government was requested to help. A Royal Commission was appointed under Lord William Amulree to study the problems of the Newfoundland economy and come up with recommendations as to how it might be improved. Among the recommendations was one that suggested Responsible Government be suspended and replaced by a commission of government which would rule until such time as Newfoundland was once again able to support itself.
3. *The Battle of Beaumont Hamel.* On 1 July 1916, the Royal Newfoundland Regiment was all but wiped out in this engagement of the first day of the Battle of the Somme. None of the Allied forces during the battle suffered as many casualties as the Regiment. When the roll was called later that day, of the 778 men who took part in the battle, only 68 answered—233 had been killed, 386 wounded and 91 were missing.
4. *The Treaty of Utrecht.* Following Queen Anne's War, in 1713, the signing of the Treaty of Utrecht granted to France fishing privileges

along a section of the Newfoundland coast that became known as the French Shore. The area took in the coast from Cape Bonavista to the tip of the Great Northern Peninsula and then south to Point Riche.

In return the French had to give up any claims on Newfoundland. This included giving up the French capital Placentia to British rule. Also the French could only remain in Newfoundland during the fishing season and could only construct buildings which would be necessary for the prosecution of the fishery.

5. *The Seven Years War/The Treaty of Paris.* The first Treaty of Paris in 1763 ended the Seven Years War and resulted in reinstatement of the terms of the Treaty of Utrecht, which gave France the right to fish along the French Shore. As well, France was given St. Pierre and Miquelon, Labrador was placed under the jurisdiction of the governor of Newfoundland, and Spain relinquished all claims to the fishery. Another spin-off was that in order to enforce the agreements of the treaty, more accurate maps and charts would have to be made. James Cook was brought in to carry out the task and created some of the first truly accurate maps of Newfoundland.

6. *The "Destroyers for Bases" agreement.* An agreement worked out between the United States and Great Britain in 1940 which gave the Royal Navy badly needed destroyers in exchange for the U.S. right to lease land on which they could build military bases in certain parts of the British Empire. The agreement gave the American Government the right to lease land in Newfoundland and Bermuda for 99 years. Construction on the Argentia Naval base was begun almost immediately, even though the official agreement was not signed until 27 March 1941. The American base at Stephenville was also begun within days of the signing.

7. *The American Revolution.* During the American Revolution the Continental Congress ruled that no goods were to be exported from the thirteen colonies to Newfoundland. To enforce the order, American privateers patrolled the Newfoundland coast. Supply ships from Britain found it difficult to break through the blockade and a lot of residents, rather than face starvation or deprivation, left Newfoundland for the American colonies. The result was a decline in the Newfoundland outports.

8. *The Navigation Acts.* These were acts of the British Parliament designed to protect Britain's interest at sea. A number of these acts had an impact on the Newfoundland fishery. In 1626 it was stipulated that fish caught by English crews must be transported to for-

eign markets in English ships. This created problems for British exporters who had worked out other arrangements with foreign importers. An outcry eventually resulted in the terms of the act being eased and eventually disregarded. Another of the acts that had an important effect on Newfoundland was the act of 1663. This one allowed for salt to be imported duty-free into North America. The ships carrying the salt often carried other goods and as the government wanted to put a halt to the black-market trade they ordered a stop. Importers argued, however, that the law didn't apply to Newfoundland because it had no civil government. Because of the difficulty in enforcing the act in Newfoundland and because the English government was more interested in stemming the problem in New England, Newfoundland continued importing and exporting illegally a number of products including refuse fish which was used to feed slaves in New York and New England, tobacco and brandy.

9. *The Treaty of Washington.* A treaty signed between the United States and Britain in 1871, whereby Newfoundland fish was given access to U.S. markets (among many other provisions). The Treaty also reinstated a part of the Reciprocity Treaty of 1854, which gave American fishermen access to Newfoundland (as well as Nova Scotia, Prince Edward Island and New Brunswick) waters. In 1885 the United States abrogated the treaty. which resulted in re-establishing duties on Newfoundland fish exports and the requirement of licences for any American vessel fishing in Canadian or Newfoundland waters.

10. *The 1894 Bank Crash.* Although a number of political and economic events led up to the crash, the event which triggered it was the death of one Mr. Hall of the London firm of Prowse, Hall and Morris on 6 December 1894. The firm, which had been serving as agent for a number of Newfoundland fish exporters, stopped business until an investigation of their own affairs could be carried out. A series of events involving English banks as well as the Commercial, Union and Savings Banks in St. John's soon cast doubt on the business practices of virtually the entire transatlantic trade in salt fish over the following weekend. On Monday 10 December the Commercial Bank kept its doors closed, as did a number of businesses which had learned the day before that they had lost their credit with banks in England. The Union Bank shut its doors after having to turn over some of its money to the Savings Bank. The result was pandemonium, resulting in the fall of the government, the collapse of several firms and the wiping out of many families' personal savings. The next year Britain sent Sir Herbert Murray as

a commissioner to distribute fishery supplies to many fishing families who could not find a merchant willing to stake them for the summer's fishery.

Early censuses

The first official census of Newfoundland was conducted in 1836. Prior to that there had been a number of other ("schemes of the fishery" and unofficial counts of the country's inhabitants.)

1522. An estimated 40-50 people, most around St. John's Harbour.

1612. Richard Whitbourne left 62 people in Newfoundland (54 men, six women, two children).

1622. Captain Edward Wynne reports that 32 people spent the winter with him at Ferryland (23 men, seven women and two boys).

1654. There were 350 families reported to be living in Newfoundland (an estimated 1750 people).

1671. A census of Placentia indicates 73 residents. In 1673 the number drops to 64.

1675. Sir John Berry's list took in the area from Cape Race to Bonavista, a total of 34 communities. By his estimate, certainly the best to that time, 1659 people were living here. There were 146 planters, 1253 fishing servants, 73 women and 187 children.

1680. Year-round settlement having been given some official sanction by Berry, a census taken by the convoy commanders reported 2181 residents.

1687. A census of nine French colonies in Newfoundland indicated 663 residents including 76 men, 44 women, 55 children and 488 servants.

The official census

1836. The first official census shows a population of 75,094.

1857. The first census to indicate a population over 100,000—124,288. This was also the first census to include Labrador.

1901. Newfoundland's population breaks the 200,000 plateau at 220,984.

1971. The number of residents reaches the half million mark at 522,104.

Family names recorded before 1670

The list of planters' names taken by Sir John Berry in 1675 is the earliest remotely reliable "census" of Newfoundland. All the family names recorded below appear in documents prior to Berry's List and continue to be present in Newfoundland at this writing.

1. Dawe (1595). As with most of the family names appearing below, the presence of the Dawe family at Port De Grave in 1595 is "backdated" from a later document. The Dawes do not, however, appear on Berry's list and may have been resident only during the fishing season in the early years.
2. Pike (1602). Gilbert Pike is said to have sailed with the pirate Peter Easton and settled in Newfoundland at Mosquito (now known as Bristol's Hope). In 1602 while serving with Easton in the Royal Navy he met and fell in love with a woman they had rescued from the Dutch. The woman was said to be an Irish Princess, Sheila Naguiera. She had been on a ship headed for France when the vessel was attacked and captured by the Dutch. The Dutch ship, in turn, was captured by Easton's men and Naguiera rescued. She and Pike were married ten days later, and when the ships arrived in Conception Bay, Pike and his bride decided to stay. Several years later Easton turned to piracy and headed for Newfoundland to recruit men. One of his stops was at Mosquito where he asked Pike to join up but Pike refused. When Easton started to raid all along the coast Pike and his family fled to Carbonear Island where they successfully defended themselves against the pirates. Eventually the Pike's settled in Carbonear, where they are honoured as founders of the town.
3. Guy (1610). John Guy's colony at Cupids began in 1610 and the following year Nicholas Guy's wife gave birth to a child, the first documented English birth in North America. Nicholas Guy (who is presumed to be some kin to the colony's governor) is later recorded to be farming in Carbonear. In John Berry's list of 1675 three Guy families are recorded at Harbour Grace and Carbonear: those of John Guy Sr, John Guy Jr, and Lewis Guy.
4. Matthews (1641). St. John's or Bay Bulls.
5. Caines (1646). St. John's.
6. Roberts (1657). St. John's.
7. Andrews (1658). Port de Grave.
8. Butler (1662). Port de Grave.

9. Earle (1662). Juggler's Cove, Bay Roberts.
10. Babcock (1663). Bay Roberts.
11. Jewer (1665). Harbour Grace.
12. Parsons (1665). Clowns Cove, Carbonear.
13. Hilliard (1666). St. John's/Bay Bulls.
14. Pearce (1668). St. John's/Bay Bulls.
15. Gordon (1669). St. John's.
16. Marshall (1670). Carbonear.
17. Fillier (1670). Port de Grave.

The Taverner and Kirke families were, with the Guys, the only extended families (three or more households) on the Island at the time of Berry's census. It is probable that the Taverner family were fishing at Bay de Verde for some years prior to 1670. There are still direct descendants bearing the family name living in the Province.

Military

Twenty significant events in Newfoundland military history

Thanks to Dr. David Facey-Crowther of MUN for his assistance on this list. Dr. Facey-Crowther has spent many years studying Newfoundland's military history.

1. 1582. The first raid against St. John's. Not against the English, but by the English. Southampton merchant Henry Oughtred attacked the Spanish fishing base in retaliation for losses he suffered in Spain.
2. 1612. Peter Easton, with nine ships and 500 men, plunders the coast of Avalon. Other raids on Newfoundland by pirates during this period caused the British Admiralty to send Sir Richard Whitbourne to investigate the problem.
3. 1618. The first mention of fortifications being built in St. John's by local inhabitants on a commanding height of land, possibly the future site of Fort William.
4. 1628. The Marquis de la Rade, with a force of three ships and 400

men cruises up and down the coast of the Avalon raiding English fishermen in St. John's and other communities. Lord Baltimore retaliates by capturing French fishing ships in Trepassey Bay and sending them home to England as prizes. This marks the beginning of a long contest between Britain and France for control of Newfoundland and the lucrative Banks fishery.
5. 1662. Placentia is settled, fortified and garrisoned by the French.
6. 1665. Christopher Martin, a Devonshire captain and vice-admiral of the Newfoundland convoy, erects a fort on the south side of the Narrows, known as the Castle.
7. 1697. Fortifications at St. John's are strengthened by the erection of a proper fort—Fort William.
8. 31 March 1698. The English Privy Council gives the order for establishing a permanent garrison at St. John's.
9. 1700. Construction begins on Fort William.
10. 1707-08. Fort William falls to a French force under St. Ovide and de Costabelle. St. John's captured and fortifications destroyed by French. The French arrived within 24 km of St. John's undetected on December 31, 1707 and at 4 AM New Year's Day attacked. Within a half hour the fight was over with only eleven casualties, 8 English soldiers and 3 French soldiers.
11. 1713. The Treaty of Utrecht. French cede Placentia and all claims to Newfoundland and St. Pierre and Miquelon. They are allowed privileges of shore bases along an area known as the "French Shore". Fortifications in St. John's allowed to decay as Placentia garrisoned by English troops.
12. 1743. Work begins on restoring fortifications of Fort William during the War of the Austrian Succession (1739-1745). Fort William garrisoned from 1745-1750 by four companies of foot.
13. 1762. On 24 June French force under Count d'Haussonville attacks St. John's receiving its surrender three days later. French improve fortifications in anticipation of an English attack. In September the English capture Torbay, then on 16 September Colonel William Amherst marches his force from Torbay directly to Quidi Vidi and then to the cliffs at Cuckold's Cove where they storm Signal Hill and capture the heights. From the heights the British bombard the French fortification which surrenders on the 18th of September. The Battle of Signal Hill was the last battle of the Seven Years War which decided the fate of France's North American Empire.
14. 1763. The English begin restoration of Fort William and construction of other installations, including the Queen's Battery on Signal

Hill. Fort Amherst, named after the English commander that captured St. John's, also commenced at this time.
15. 1773-79. The construction of Fort Townshend and Military Road.
16. 1775-76. Newfoundlanders participate in defence of Quebec against attack by American generals Benedict Arnold and Richard Montgomery.
17. 1791. The Quidi Vidi Battery, abandoned in 1784, is repaired and guards eastern approaches to Signal Hill. Throughout the Napoleonic Wars it is a part of the defences of St. John's.
18. 1792-93. Captain Thomas Skinner of the Royal Engineers raises four companies of volunteers at his own expense, known as the Royal Newfoundland Volunteers.
19. 1795. Skinner granted permission to raise a regiment of fencible infantry, later known as the Royal Newfoundland Regiment.
20. 1 July 1916. The Newfoundland Regiment is virtually annihilated at Battle of Beaumont Hamel.

Eight Newfoundland battles

1. 1585. Bernard Drake's capture of the Portuguese fleet. In command of the *Golden Riall*, Drake and George Raymond captured several Spanish and Portuguese fishing vessels in Bay Bulls. Then they moved on to the Azores and captured more of the fleet. Drake was knighted for his services, but was brought to trial for his treatment of a number of Portuguese prisoners. During the trial the Judge, eight J.P.s and 11 of the 12 jurors contracted an infection from the Portuguese and died. Drake, himself, contracted the disease and died on 10 April 1586.
2. 1665. A Dutch raid on St. John's. Admiral de Ruyter said after the raid that had there been six mounted guns he would not have attempted the attack.
3. 1696-97. D'Iberville's raid. In the autumn of 1696 Pierre Le Moyne d'Iberville was sent to drive the English out of Newfoundland. His campaign resulted in almost the total destruction of English settlements in the colony. Only Bonavista and Carbonear Island survived.
4. 1697. The defence of Carbonear Island. When d'Iberville attacked Carbonear on 24 January 1697, residents retreated to Carbonear Island. Attempts by the French to get the English settlers to surrender were in vain and eventually the French returned to Placentia.
5. 1703. The English Blockade of Placentia. During the War of the Spanish Succession the British fleet blockaded Placentia harbour, preventing supply ships from arriving with stores for the residents.

The blockade resulted in half the population starving to death.
6. 1704. Michael Gill's defence of Bonavista. Gill was a New England-based merchant. On 28 August 1704 he was in Bonavista when the French attacked. He rallied the residents of the community and successfully held off the attackers.
7. 1762. The Battle of Signal Hill. The last battle of the Seven Years War in North America.
8. 1942. U-boat attacks. Attacks in September and November on ore ships at Bell Island resulted in the sinking of four ships and 69 fatalities. On 13 October, the U-69 torpedoed and sank the ferry *Caribou*, resulting in the loss of 137 lives.

Five foreign battlefield parks which honour Newfoundlanders who fought in World War I

These parks commemorate battles in which the Royal Newfoundland Regiment played a significant role.

1. Monchy-Le-Proux, France.
2. Masnieres, France (Battle of Cambrai).
3. Gueudecourt, France.
4. Beaumont Hamel, France.
5. Courtrai, Belgium.

The parks were designed by Rudolf H. Cochius (who also designed Bowring Park). Each features a statue of a caribou, the Regiment's emblem—all were the work of Basil Gotto, who also sculpted the caribou in Bowring Park.

Disasters

The 13 most tragic marine disasters in Newfoundland waters

The sinking of the *Titanic*, on 12 April 1914, was not exactly in "Newfoundland waters," but on the Grand Banks 409 nautical miles from Cape Race. 1522 people died when the passenger liner, thought to be unsinkable, struck an iceberg.

1. *Anglo Saxon.* 27 April 1863—237 died when a steamer carrying British emigrants to Canada sank in fog at Clam Cove, on the Southern Shore of the Avalon Peninsula. There were 209 survivors.
2. *Harpooner.* 2 November 1816—206 people perished when this British transport ship went on the rocks at Marine Cove, St. Shotts.
3. The *Pollux* and *Truxtun*. 18 February 1942—the *Pollux*, an American troop carrier, and the *Truxtun*, a supply ship, ran aground at Chamber Cove and sank. 186 servicemen were rescued by residents of St. Lawrence and Lawn, but there were 193 fatalities.
4. *Southern Cross.* 31 March 1914—173 sealers died when the *Southern Cross* sank during a fierce storm. This is one of the great mysteries of Newfoundland marine history. When last seen at St. Mary's Bay she was headed full steam for St. John's. The ship simply disappeared with no trace of bodies or wreckage.
5. *Caribou.* 13 October 1942—a Port aux Basques-Sydney ferry, torpedoed by the German submarine U-69 (nicknamed "The Laughing Cow" by her crew). 137 passengers and crew perished.
6. *Florizel.* 24 February 1918—94 passengers and crew died when Bowrings' steamer sank near Renews.
7. *Ocean Ranger.* 15 February 1982—84 crew members died when the semi-submersible drill rig sank during a fierce storm about 300 km off Newfoundland.
8. *Newfoundland.* March 1918—most of the crew perished on the ice after being separated from the vessel during a storm. 78 men died.
9. *Monasco.* 21 July 1857—55 people died in one of the more mysterious stories about disaster at sea. After the ship sank, near Corbin Head on the Burin Peninsula, there were rumours which suggested that the captain and a wife of one of the passengers killed everyone on board.
10. *Lion.* 6 January 1882—52 people perished. The ship is thought to have exploded.
11. *Greenland.* 21 March 1898—48 men died after a sudden storm left sealers stranded on the ice and separated from their ship.
12. *Huntsman.* 23 April 1873—44 crewmen died when this sealing ship was lost at the ice.
13. *Viking.* 15 March 1931—the *Viking* was on her way north to shoot some extra scenes for a feature movie. The movie's director Varrick Frizzel was among the passengers. It is said that he and one of the crew were just discussing the placement of a warning sign about explosives on board when the dynamite blew, near the Horse Islands. Frizzel was among the 27 people lost.

Three notable aviation disasters

1. *Arrow Air*—16 December 1985. 263 people died when this DC-10, carrying American servicemen back to the United States, crashed just after takeoff from Gander International Airport. Although the cause of the crash was initially believed to have been icing, many experts disputed that theory, and even speculated that it may have been caused by a terrorist's bomb. The true cause remains shrouded in controversy.
2. *The Banting crash*—21 February 1941. Although only two people died in the crash of this Hudson Bomber near Musgrave Harbour, it is significant because of the death of one of the passengers, Dr. Frederick Grant Banting, who with Charles Best discovered insulin.
3. *Sabena*—16 September 1946. 26 of the 44 passengers and crew on board died when a Sabena DC-4 enroute from Brussels to New York via Gander crashed 22 miles south-south-west of Gander Airport. At the time it was the biggest airline disaster in history.

Two tsunami

1. The Lisbon Earthquake. In 1755 a mid-Atlantic earthquake wreaked disaster in the Portuguese capital. Cape Bonavista experienced unusually high seas, when Bonavista harbour suddenly was completely drained. Ten minutes later, the sea returned, flooding much of the town. A well-known folksong, "Great big sea hove in Long Beach," recounts the incident.
2. The Burin Peninsula Tidal Wave. 18 November 1929—the sea drained from harbours on the Burin Peninsula only to return, causing 27 people deaths and untold damage to fishing stages, homes and businesses. The damage to the seabed caused a general failure in the local fishery for the next few years.

Famous fires

1. The Great St. John's Fires. St. John's has probably had more fires causing great destruction than any other major commercial centre in North America. Three of them have become known as "Great Fires:" 1817, 1846 and 1892. The 1817 Fire was actually two fires, one on November 7, the other on November 21. (An earlier fire in February, 1816 compounded the effects of the 1817 blaze.) In total almost 400 buildings were consumed and a quarter of the population was left homeless.

The Great Fire of 1846 began on George Street when a pot of glue ignited. By the time the blaze ended all the major merchant houses were destroyed along with the Court House, the Church of England cathedral, the customs house and several other important buildings. The Fire of 1892 was the most devastating of all the fires. It was caused by embers from Tommy Fitzpatrick's lit pipe dropped on some dry hay at Tim O'Brien's stable at the junction of Pennywell and Freshwater Roads. This blaze virtually destroyed the city with a total loss estimated at 13 million dollars.

And these were only the major conflagrations in St. John's. Others included fires set by the French in their attacks on the city as well as the fires of 1833, 1838, 1855 and others.

2. The Harbour Grace Fire. On 18 August 1832 a fire destroyed much of the town's commercial district along with Keef's Hotel, The Waterford Arms, St. Paul's Church, The Parsonage and Newfoundland School, and other major public building and mercantile premises. At least a hundred families lost their homes.
3. The Knights of Columbus Hostel. On 12 December 1942, 99 people (many of them servicemen) died in a fire which engulfed the Knights of Columbus hostel on Harvey Road in St. John's. Speculation was that the fire had been set by a saboteur.
4. Woody Point. In 1922 the entire business district in this Bonne Bay community was wiped out by a fire which claimed 58 buildings and several wharves.
5. Glenwood. In 1901 a fire at a mill owned by the Glenwood Lumber Company burned the structure to the ground before it had a chance to process a single log. The townsite was also wiped out in the blaze. Another blaze in 1919 destroyed the town and many people were evacuated by train.
6. The Hull House Fire. On 10 February 1948 a fire swept through a nursing home owned by Isaac Hull in downtown St. John's. Thirty four people died in a blaze that had been started by a faulty oil stove.
7. Chafe's Nursing Home. On Boxing Day in 1976 a fire broke out at Chafe's Nursing Home in the Gould's. Twenty one people died in the blaze.
8. The Forest Fires of 1961. During the summer of 1961 a total of 309 forest fires broke out in Newfoundland. Bonavista North was especially hard hit by the fires. Several communities had to be evacuated by sea, as any escape by land was impossible because of the raging blaze. By September over a million acres had been burned and numerous people had lost their homes and possessions.
9. The Forest Fires of 1904—another year in which Newfoundlanders

suffered tremendously because of forest fires. The blazes raged from the Bay of Islands all the way to the east coast during a hot, dry summer. In evaluating the damage caused by the fires, officials decided that they couldn't depend on rain alone to fight forest fires and appointed a Chief Woods Ranger and support staff. In 1910 a Fire Patrol was established to protect the forests and fight fires along the railway lines.

Natural History

Rare bird sightings

Newfoundland is a birders paradise, because of the numbers and variety which stop off here on their migrations. The following is a list of confirmed sightings on the Island of birds which were far outside their normal ranges—including a pair of flamingos sighted at Sops Arm in 1977! My thanks to Bill Montevecchi of MUN for assisting with the following two bird lists.

Loons: Pacific/Arctic Loon.
Pelicans: American White Pelican.
Frigatebirds: Magnificent Frigatebird.
Herons: Little Egret & Tricolored Heron.
Ibises: White Ibis.
Flamingos: Greater Flamingo.
Swans, Geese & Ducks: Tundra Swan, Pink-footed Goose, Barnacle Goose, Gadwall, Canvasback, Redhead and Tufted Duck.
American Vultures: Turkey Vulture.
Ospreys, Eagles & Hawks: Cooper's Hawk.
Rails, Gallinules & Coots: Corn Crake, Clapper Rail, King Rail and Eurasian Coot.
Cranes: Sandhill Crane.
Plovers: Common Ringed Plover.
Stilts: Black-necked Stilt.
Auks: Marbled Murrelet.
Owls: Barn Owl and Long-eared Owl.
Goatsuckers: Chuck-will's-widow.
Hummingbirds: Rufous Hummingbird.
Woodpeckers: Lewis' Woodpecker.

Tyrant Flycatchers: Eastern Phoebe, Say's Phoebe, Great Crested Flycatcher.
Jays, Magpies & Crows: Black-billed Magpie.
Wrens: House Wren.
Old World Warblers & Thrushes: Townsend's Solitaire, Fieldfare and Redwing.
Vireos: Yellow-throated Vireo.
Wood Warblers, Tanagers, Sparrows & Blackbirds: Golden-winged Warbler, Yellow-rumped "Audubon's" Warbler and Townsend's Warbler.

Hypothetical bird list for Newfoundland

Eight Newfoundland sightings of birds that are assumed to be genuine, but where there is not enough information to consider the sightings confirmed.

1. Yellow-nosed Albatross.
2. Little Shearwater.
3. Roseate Tern.
4. Pileated Woodpecker.
5. Eastern Bluebird.
6. LeConte's Sparrow.
7. Brewer's Blackbird.
8. Orchard Oriole.

Peter Scott's ten facts about Newfoundland and Labrador plants

Thanks to Dr. Peter Scott, of MUN's Botanical Garden and a frequent contributor to CBC Radio's "Crosstalk on Gardening" feature for this list.

1. The blueberry family, Ericaceae, is our most important family of shrubs and is represented everywhere in the province.
2. The oldest trees on the Island are the tuckamores found around the coast. Many are 80 years or older.
3. The pitcher plant, our provincial emblem, was chosen by Queen Victoria. As it is a carnivorous plant, it supplements its nutrient requirements by capturing insects.
4. The Island of Newfoundland has 1267 different species of plants, while Labrador has 674 species. In all there are about 1300 different species in the entire province.

5. A number of plants reach their northern or southern limit of distribution in Newfoundland and Labrador.
6. Diapensia, an Alpine plant, is in the process of evolving into two species on the Island.
7. A plant common in Eurasia, the straw coloured orchid (Plantanthera albida var. straminea), has one known population in North America, at L'Anse aux Meadows.
8. One of the most widespread plants in the world is the bracken fern, a common plant on the Island.
9. The cow parsnip can reach gigantic proportions; 9 feet or a bit more.
10. Alders heal scars on the landscape. They have root nodules where nitrogen, an essential nutrient, is captured from the air. This allows them to grow on really poor sites.

Jim Butler's interesting geological formations

For this informed list (and a list of mines which follows) I am indebted to Jim Butler of the Geological Survey division of the provincial Department of Mines and Energy. If you'd like more information about the geological features of Newfoundland and Labrador, take a look at the division's World Wide Web Page: **http://www.geosurv.gov.nf.ca**

1. *The Arches.* Located on the west side of the Great Northern Peninsula, a few miles north of the community of Parsons Pond, a large block of limestone, about 50 feet high, has been separated from the coastal rock by wave action. Two arches, which were at one time caves in the block, are exposed just within reach of the ocean. Provincial parks has marked the area with signs along the highway and has constructed a trail to the beach so that it is readily accessible.
2. *The Spout.* A crevasse in the rocky shore south of Bay Bulls, which for years sent a spray of seawater into the air with each wave, was stopped by idle individuals several years ago. A large boulder was dropped into the crevasse and became wedged in place, thus stopping the water from spraying. In 1995 members of the East Coast Trail Association, and interested citizens of the area, aided by a group of army engineers, were successful in removing the boulder and put The Spout back in operation.
3. *The Dungeon.* A huge sea cave that collapsed several hundred years ago is a place of interest near the tip of the Bonavista Peninsula. The Dungeon began as a couple of crevasses along the coast. Over thousands of years, the ocean wore away the rock where it was soft or weakened by fractures, creating a cavern that was connected by

two sea caves. The cavern became so large that the roof over it could not be supported and it collapsed into itself.

Continuing wave action removed most of the material and today a huge hole, about 250 metes in diameter and 15 metres deep, connected to the ocean by two sea caves (or sea tunnels) now exist. Provincial parks has provided an interpretative sign and parking at the site, located just off the road leading to the Cape Bonavista lighthouse.

4. *Western Brook Pond*. Although you might not think about it as an ocean-formed feature, the fjord that forms present-day Western Brook Pond, in Gros Morne National Park, is also the work of a combination of the action of ocean waves and the huge sheet of ice that covered Newfoundland several thousand years ago. Although this feature is located several miles from the coast today, it was at one time an intricate part of our coastline. As the weight of the mile-thick sheet of ice was removed by melting, the land rebounded, moving the fiord inland. The Fjord is located at the north end of Gros Morne National Park. The National Park service has allowed the site to be developed as a tourist attraction and a scheduled boat tour is available at that location.

Other fiords, along the south coast of the Island, and in the northern parts of Labrador, are still accessible from the sea and make a spectacular sight from the deck of a small pleasure craft or a large yacht. Not all the geological features of Newfoundland were created by ocean waves, but oceans have played a part in their creation. For example:

5. *The Tablelands*. A feature located in the Trout River area of Gros Morne National Park, this extensive flat-topped range of hills is reminiscent of a desolate moonscape. These rocks are the remnants of ocean-floor material that was brought to the surface when the proto-Atlantic Ocean closed about 470 million years ago, during the Ordovician period. They consist of ultramafic rock, a rock type that constitutes the Earth's upper mantle. This area has a eerie appearance because of the yellow-orange colour of the rocks and the lack of extensive vegetation. The ultramafic rocks contain many elements that inhibit plant growth and contrast sharply with the more abundant vegetation on the north side of the highway. This is yet another site that emphasises Newfoundland's important place in the study of global geology.

6. *The Hole in the Wall*. To the south of Pinsent's Arm, on the south coast of Labrador, is a feature known as the Hole in the Wall. A weak zone of rock has been eroded by the combination of wave-ac-

tion and the "freeze-thaw" cycle of water, to create a hole in the cliff face. This hole extends through the cliff to a valley on the other side of the cliff. As ships pass this point it is possible to see the vegetation on the valley wall behind through the hole.

7. *The Dover Fault.* This is a major break in the Earth's crust, which takes its name from the town of Dover, Bonavista Bay. On the eastern side ancient volcanic rocks of the ancient continent of Gondwana are exposed; to the west, continental rocks are buried beneath younger sedimentary rocks that formed in the proto-Atlantic Ocean (also known as the Iapetus Ocean). The surface expression of the fault is a low area or notch between higher more resistant rock on either side. It is probably best viewed from the town of Hare Bay's municipal park.

8. *The Porcupine Strand.* A magnificent white sandy beach, extending for 35 km north and south of Cape Porcupine, near the entrance to Groswater Bay, Labrador. The sand was derived from sand and gravel deposited inland by glaciers about 10,000 years ago. Black sand layers within the beach deposits consist of magnetite, ilmenite and other heavy minerals concentrated by wave-action.

9. *The Quaker Hat.* An isolated island that is shaped like a broad-brimmed hat, near Cape Harrison, Labrador. The hat is complete with a black band around the base of the crown. The "band" is a gabbro sill (a dark, medium-grained intrusive rock) which intrudes the overlying granitic rocks.

10. *The Corner Brook Caves.* Located just off the TransCanada Highway, a few kilometres south of the City of Corner Brook, these caves were carved out of limestone by the action of the water of Corner Brook Stream. The caves are a few hundred feet deep and vary in height from 3-8 feet. The cave system is accessible at times of low water. Debris has blocked part of the cave system several hundred feet from the entrance.

11. *American Men.* Among the coastal islands, and in particular between Black Tickle and Snug Harbour, Labrador, the most prominent peaks are crowned by stone markers or cairns. These were erected by native peoples and early Europeans as an aid to navigation in bad weather. Some of these markers have existed for hundreds of years. They are known as American Men. Some think that this may be a corruption of Marker Men, or they may reflect the influence of early American whalers along this coast.

12. *The Devil's Dancing Table.* At Henley Harbour, on the coast of Labrador, is a very large, flat-topped rock feature. The cap rock is massive basalt whereas the lower layers are an older and thicker

basalt which developed vertical cracks during cooling. From a distance, this feature has the appearance of a table supported by a multitude of legs. Locally this feature is called Castles Hill.

Extra-terrestrial objects

Jim Butler also provided a list of features in the Province that have nothing to do with oceans, wave action or erosion, but have an extra-terrestrial influence.

1. *The Buchans Meteor.*Many people will remember the brilliant flash of light that extinguished the street lights in the town of Buchans on 19 January 1986. A brilliant meteor streaked across the early evening sky, travelling in a south-southwest direction. A few days later, two hunters reported finding an area that had been disturbed by what they thought might be a meteorite impact in the vicinity of Lake Ahwachanjeesh, north of the community of St. Alban's, Bay d'Espoir, southern Newfoundland.

   Investigations by geologists of the Geological Survey of the Provincial Department of Mines and Energy, discovered evidence of an impact in the area but did not uncover the meteorite.

2. *Mistastin Lake.* The largest known meteor crater in the Province is about 120 kilometres west of Davis Inlet. Shown on the maps as Mistastin Lake, it has a central uplift island and rim. Shatter cones (fractures in the rock which are diagnostic of high-speed impacts), shock metamorphosed minerals and other indications of meteor impact is associated with the area.

3. *Merewether Crater.* A second such area occurs about 100 kilometres west of Hebron, in northern Labrador.

   The crater is much smaller, only about 200 metres in diameter, and much younger than the one at Mistastin Lake. Known as the Merewether crater (named after the American airman who first sighted the crater in the 1940s), this crater occurs in an area of bouldery till. Shock metamorphic minerals have recently been discovered at this site, which confirms it origins as an impact crater.

Although no impact craters have been discovered on the Island of Newfoundland, there are conical fractures (similar to "shatter cones") have been reported from bedrock near the Health Science Complex in St. John's. Some scientists suggest that they may be the remains of an ancient (now eroded) impact crater.

Fossil finds

This list of accessible fossil locations was provided by Doug Boyce of Geological Surveys

1. *Kelligrews Quarries*, Red Bridge Road, Conception Bay South. Early to middle Cambrian trilobites, brachiopods and hyolithids.
2. *Bell Island*. Abundant early Ordovician trace fossils.
3. *Big Salmonier Brook* (Burin Peninsula), south shore of mouth. Middle Cambrian trilobites.
4. *Elliot's Cove* (Random Island), shoreline to the south of the community.
5. *New World Island*. Trilobites, ostracodes, brachiopods, bivalves, cephalopods, gastropods, corals, bryozoans and graptolites.
6. *Red Cliff Overpass* (near Grand Falls). Ordovician graptolites.
7. *Lower Cove* (Port au Port Peninsula), east side. Early Ordovician trilobites, ostracodes, brachiopods, cephalopods, gastropods and crinoids.
8. *Piccadilly Quarry* (Port au Port Peninsula). Middle Ordovician trilobites, ostracodes, brachiopods, cephalopods, gastropods, crinoids and graptolites.
9. *Aguathuna Quarry* (Port au Port Peninsula). Middle Ordovician trilobites, ostracodes, brachiopods, cephalopods, gastropods and crinoids, early Carboniferous tube worms, brachiopods and bivalves.
10. *Eddies Cove West* (Great Northern Peninsula). Early Ordovician trilobites, ostracodes, brachiopods, cephalopods, gastropods, crinoids and graptolites.
11. *Boat Harbour to Cape Norman* (Great Northern Peninsula). Early Ordovician trilobites, ostracodes, brachiopods, cephalopods, gastropods and crinoids.
12. *Blanc Sablon, Quebec to Point Amour, Labrador* (roadside shales exposures). Early Cambrian trilobites.
13. *Redmonds Pit* (western Labrador). Cretaceous insect wings and plant fossils. These fossils are contemporary with the age of dinosaurs and are possibly worth checking for dinosaur bone fragments. Dinosaur bones were reportedly drilled through in the course of oil exploration on the Grand Banks, but these fossils could hardly be considered accessible!

Abandoned mines worth a visit

As a further attraction to the "geological tourist," Newfoundland has its fair share of abandoned mines. Some were active in the 1800s others more recently abandoned. Here is a list of such mines, as provided by Jim Butler, together with their location, period of operation and the mineral mined.

All these old minesites can be visited and prove to be interesting areas for collecting mineral specimens.

1. *Fleur de Lys*. At the north end of the community of Fleur de Lys on the Baie Verte Peninsula is an outcrop of soapstone, where Paleoeskimos quarried soapstone blocks to use as bowls and lamps—between 1100 and 1600 years ago!
2. *Shoal Bay Mine*. South of St. John's, this copper mine was Newfoundland's first producing mine, being operated by Cornish miners between 1776 and 1778. Although it deserves to be visited for historic reasons, there is little of interest remaining of the mine itself. Watch out for ghosts, however!
3. *Tilt Cove*. On route 414, Baie Verte Peninsula, Tilt Cove was one of Newfoundland most successful mines (1864-1917 and 1957-67). There remain numerous pits and adits, smelter sites and waste piles, as well as many signs of mineralization (copper) and mining activity.
4. *Aguathuna*. At the isthmus of the Port au Port Peninsula, Aguathuna was an open-pit operation for quarrying limestone, to use as a flux for the steelmaking facilities at North Sydney, Nova Scotia. It operated between 1913 and 1966. The interesting shapes carved into the limestone by the ocean appeal to the more romantic visitor, while the old quarry and loading facilities appeal to the "industrial archaeologist."
5. *Pilley's Island Pyrite Mine*. This was an iron sulphide (pyrite) with copper mine. Some old mine workings can be seen within the community of Pilley's Island, especially around Mine Pond, and in the hills above Bumblebee Bight. This was the first mine in Newfoundland to install electric lights and operated between 1887 and 1908.
6. *Sleepy Cove Mine*. At Crow Head, Twillingate, the mine site is now Sea Breeze Municipal Park—including a small adit. This copper mine operated only for a few years in the late 1800s. Specimens of quartz crystals and pyrite can be obtained.
7. *LaManche, Placentia Bay*. Remnants of this galena (lead) mine include an adit on the beach, some trenches, waste piles and a partially sealed shaft. There are collectible samples in several old dumps. Operated from 1850 to 1900.
8. *Moreton's Harbour Mine*. Near Little Harbour, Notre Dame Bay,

remnants of this antimony mine (from 1892-1916) include some trenches, waste piles with good specimens, and a water-filled shaft.
9. *Silver Cliff Mine.* Near Argentia, lead with some silver. Machinery and shafts are remnants of operations 1880-95 and 1922-1925.
10. *Bell Island.* Collectible specimens of sedimentary iron ore or hematite (and good fossils as well) at several locations. There are numerous stockpiles of ore and ore waste and several adits that have been sealed. Operated from 1895 to 1966.

Business and Engineering

The oldest businesses in Newfoundland

Seven businesses in the Province that have been around for 150 years or more

1. Harvey and Company (established 1767 as the Bermuda Trading Company).
2. Baine, Johnston and Co. (1780, as Robert Baine & Co.).
3. T.B. Clift (1790, as Clift, Wood and Co.).
4. Bowring Brothers (1811, as Benjamin Bowring & Sons).
5. Carnell's Funeral Home (1835, as Carnell's Carriage Works).
6. Dicks & Co. (1840).
7. Muir's Marble Works (1842).

Some more businesses that are at least 100 years old

1. Steers Ltd. (established 1858).
2. A. Harvey & Company (1865).
3. John Quinton Ltd. of Red Cliff, Bonavista Bay (1870).
4. T & M Winter (1878).
5. The *Evening Telegram* (1879).
6. Johnson Insurance (1880).
7. Newfoundland Light and Power (1885, originally the St. John's Electric Light Co.).
8. P.C. O'Driscoll (1888).
9. J.T. Swyers, Bonavista (1892).
10. Robinson-Blackmore (1894).

11. Munn and Co. of Harbour Grace and St. John's (1895).
12. W.J. Murphy, a St. John's corner grocery (1895).
13. Henry J. Thomas (1895, continuing a contracting business started by Thomas's father in 1856).

Ten man-made marvels

1. The Bull Arm Project and construction of the Hibernia platform.
2. The Newfoundland Railway.
3. Churchill Falls.
4. Goose Air Base.
5. The Upper Salmon-Bay d'Espoir hydro development.
6. The transatlantic telegraph cable landed at Heart's Content.
7. The Grand Falls paper mill.
8. The Corner Brook paper mill.
9. The completion of the Trans-Canada Highway.
10. The Carol Project, Labrador City.

Religion

Hans Rollmann's ten significant events in Newfoundland and Labrador religious history

1. 5000 BC: Burial artifacts such as bird bone and walrus tusk in a grave at L'Anse-Amour indicate a close relationship between religion and nature among the Maritime Archaic Indians.
2. 1639: Sir David Kirke promises Archbishop Laud in a letter from Ferryland that, unlike the American settlements to the south, his Avalon plantation would be a model of "happy conformity" to the Church of England. Already Sir Humphrey Gilbert had in 1583 proclaimed in St. John's harbour that "religion in public exercise should be according to the Church of England."
3. 1771: A party of Moravians, among them Christoph Brasen, Jens Haven and Christian Drachardt and three women, establish Nain as their first missionary station and headquarters.
4. 1775: Congregationalism is introduced to Newfoundland by the Reverend John Jones, a former paymaster in the St. John's garrison, against much official opposition. Jones converted to evangelical

Christianity when he saw a fellow-soldier, mortally wounded in a duel, curse God.
5. 1784: Governor John Campbell, the son of a Scottish Presbyterian clergyman, publicly announces religious liberty to all inhabitants of Newfoundland, including Roman Catholics. Later, Campbell would also defend the religious rights of Congregationalists and Methodists.
6. 1839: Queen Victoria creates Newfoundland, together with Bermuda, into an Anglican episcopal see and appoints her relative George Aubrey Spencer, the archdeacon of Bermuda, as its first bishop.
7. 1885: Newfoundlander Emma Churchill, and her husband Charles Dawson, two honeymooners, bring the Salvation Army message to Portugal Cove. Eventually, the socially-concerned religious holiness group achieves the largest per capita Salvationist presence in any Canadian province.
8. 1904: St. John's becomes a Roman Catholic archdiocese after 120 years of continuous religious presence on the island, and Michael Francis Howley, the first Roman Catholic bishop born in Newfoundland, is elevated to the rank of archbishop.
9. 1910: Alice Belle Garrigus, an American Pentecostal preacher, arrives in St. John's and establishes Bethesda Mission, the first congregation of what eventually would become the Pentecostal Assemblies of Newfoundland and Labrador. The Pentecostals, whose strength can be found especially in central and western Newfoundland, are the fastest growing contemporary religious body in the province.
10. 1925: By an act of the Newfoundland legislature, Newfoundland Methodists become officially part of the United Church of Canada. Methodism was first introduced into Conception Bay in 1766 by the Reverend Laurence Coughlan, a former lay preacher of John Wesley and later a clergyman in Lady Huntingdon's Connexion.

Sports

I am the first to admit that I know little about sports. One of the observations about my last two books of trivia was the lack of sports information, so I was determined this time around to address that. I called on the assistance of the most sports-informed person I knew, Steve O'Brien. Steve does the sports trivia call-in feature on CBC'S Radio Noon, and is the sports trivia columnist for the *Evening Telegram*. I keep telling Steve he should write a book of Newfoundland and Labrador sports trivia. Maybe, this will prove the incentive he needs: I merely asked Steve to provide lists of moments in sport, great teams and significant athletes. He did the rest. In fact, to make sure he was leaving nothing out (and to verify some of the facts), Steve called on a few experts himself: the *Evening Telegram*'s sports staff, Carl Lake, George McClaren, Doug Redmond and Dee Murphy.

Steve limited himself to significant people and events in Newfoundland sports history since 1949. Factors such as provincial and/or national titles won and length of playing career were considered in the selection process. Also, an attempt was made to acknowledge athletes throughout the Province, as well as those who compete in individual sports that often are not given a high profile.

Ten great Newfoundland and Labrador sports teams

1. *St. Lawrence Laurentians and Holy Cross Crusaders soccer teams* (tie): To show how dominant these two teams have been in provincial senior soccer competition, over the 30-year span from 1967 to 1996, there have only been six occasions when a team other than Holy Cross or St. Lawrence has won the Challenge Cup, the symbol of soccer supremacy in Newfoundland. St. Lawrence has 13 titles to their credit, while the Crusaders have 11. In addition, Holy Cross had an incredible streak of 17 consecutive titles in the St. John's senior league (1978-94), captured the national Challenge Cup in 1988 and were runner-up the following season. Given the relatively small population on the soccer-mad Burin Peninsula, it is a remarkable achievement that the Laurentians have been so good for so long.
3. *The 1970-71 Grand Falls Cataracts:* This is the only team ever to lose the first three games of the Herder Trophy finals, yet come back to win the championship. The Cataracts played the defending champions St. John's Capitals in the best-of-seven final that year, and were largely written off when they dropped the first two games

on home ice. Led by the spectacular goaltending of Jean-Guy Morrisette and helped by some timely scoring, the Cats roared back to take the Herder, winning the final games on the Capitals' home ice. To prove it was no fluke, they won again the next season.

4. *The 1981 Smith-Stockley rowing crew* that broke the 80-year old course record at the Royal St. John's Regatta. In 1901 a group of Outer Cove fishermen rowed the course at Quidi Vidi Lake in a time of 9:13.8 (or 9:13 4/5). By the 1960s, many observers felt that the time would never be broken, but in the late 1970s some crews felt that the time was within reach. At the 1981 Regatta (August 5), the Smith-Stockley rowers won the Club Race in a time of 9:12.04, beating the long-standing record and climaxing five years of intense training. Coxed by "Skipper" Jim Ring, members of the winning crew were: Paul and Randy Ring (Jim's sons), Bill Holwell, Brian Cranford, Tom Power and John Barrington. Even though the current course record is under nine minutes, the satisfaction of breaking "the time of 9:13" makes the 1981 accomplishment particularly noteworthy.

5. *The 1948-59 St. Bon's senior hockey team.* This club was a powerhouse in hockey for several decades, not only as a St. John's-based club team, but also as a provincial champion. In fact, St. Bon's *twice* won the Herder Trophy five years in a row, prior to Newfoundland becoming a province of Canada. The 1948-59 squad make the list, however, due to their 12-year run as Boyle Trophy champions (the prize for the top team in the now-defunct St. John's city league). There were not many artificial ice rinks in Newfoundland prior to Confederation, but students of St. Bon's were fortunate to have ready access to their own facility, the Forum. "Practice makes perfect" as the saying goes, and the school hockey teams certainly worked on their game. Many of the athletes in the provincial Sports Hall of Fame played hockey for St. Bon's during this period. Ted Withers, Ed Manning, Bill and Ted Gillies, and Hugh Fardy are just some of the players that helped comprise the St. Bon's dynasty, and all have been enshrined in the provincial Sports Hall of Fame.

6. *The 1955-59 Grand Falls Andcos hockey team.* The Andcos (from the Anglo-Newfoundland Development Company) are the only Newfoundland senior team since Confederation to win the Herder Trophy five consecutive seasons. The paper company built the Grand Falls Stadium, brought in an excellent coach (Joe Byrne) and made a strong commitment to the team, all of which resulted in a great deal of success on the ice.

7. *St. John's Shamrocks senior baseball team.* For nine straight sea-

sons (1980-88), Shamrocks were the top team in the highly competitive St. John's senior league. Although their streak was broken in 1989, the Shammies have continued to win championships in the 1990s. In addition, a strong junior program is helping to maintain the club as one of Newfoundland's premiere baseball franchises.

8. *Williams Brothers' rowing crew* (Harbour Grace Regatta): The accomplishments of this team of rowers have largely gone unrecognized outside of the Carbonear-Harbour Grace area, but certainly deserve province-wide recognition. From 1960-68, the Williams team won the championship race at the Harbour Grace Regatta nine straight years. In 1974, the brothers came out of retirement in an attempt to win their tenth title, and proved they were equal to the task. Since this regatta dates back to the 1860s, and no other crew has seriously challenged this winning streak, their domination of the event is truly impressive. Clayton, David, Fred, Gordon, Kevin and Leonard Williams are worthy champions and merit strong consideration as one of the province's best—but least known—sports teams.

9. *1995 MUN Sea-Hawks ladies basketball team*: Memorial captured the AUAA (Atlantic Universities Athletic Association) championship for the first time in 1995, upsetting several schools with strong basketball programs. In addition, MUN's Michelle Healey won the MVP award for the season, climaxing a campaign that helped to elevate womens' basketball in this province to a higher level.

10. *Sue-Ann Bartlett's curling rink*. This foursome from Labrador City has been a dominant factor on both the Newfoundland and Canadian curling scenes for the past 20 years. The Bartlett rink has represented the province with distinction numerous times at the Scott Tournament of Hearts Canadian championship, advancing to the finals on one occasion. The rink is among the career leaders in games won at the national tournament, and today remains active in provincial and national seniors' events.

Ten great moments in Newfoundland and Labrador sports history

1. *Alex Faulkner becomes the first Newfoundlander to play in the NHL*: On 7 December 1961, Alex Faulkner from Bishop's Falls suited up for the Toronto Maple Leafs in a game at the historic Montreal Forum, and instantly became a celebrity throughout the Province. That was his only game for Toronto, as he was acquired by the Detroit Red Wings in time for the 1962-63 NHL season. In

the Stanley Cup playoffs that spring, Faulkner scored game-winning goals against Chicago and Toronto before the Leafs ultimately prevailed. Though his NHL career was relatively short (less than two seasons), Alex Faulkner was the only Newfoundlander to play in the "original six" era when there were only 120 roster positions available (400 less than today.) Because his stint in the NHL was followed so closely by so many Newfoundlanders (even those who weren't hockey fans), it remains a milestone event in Newfoundland's sports' history.

2. *St. John's plays host to the 1977 Canada Summer Games*: From 7-19 August 1977, the attention of many Canadians was focused on Newfoundland, as the province played host to the third Canada Summer Games. Although the athletic events were held in the capital city, the Games' staff, volunteers, and our provincial team were from the entire province. Besides leaving many athletic facilities still in use today, the Games proved to be a great advertisement for both Newfoundland hospitality and our ability to host such large-scale competitions. The athletic highlight was swimmer Blair Tucker's gold medal for the province in the 200-metre butterfly event. Nearly 3000 spectators (myself included) jammed into the Aquarena, while a great many more watched on national television to see the first Canada Games gold medal performance by a Newfoundlander. The 1977 Canada Summer Games in St. John's were an unqualified success in terms of competition and fan support. More importantly, they served to boost Newfoundlanders' pride and self-esteem in achieving such a measure of success on a national stage.

3. *Holy Cross soccer team wins the national Challenge Cup*: In the midst of their domination of the St. John's soccer league from 1978-94, Holy Cross represented the province at the 1988 national Challenge Cup tournament hosted that year by British Columbia. After a considerable fund-raising effort to finance the trip, the Crusaders returned home with the nation's top soccer award. Not only did the team go undefeated, but also did not allow a goal during the tournament, quite an accomplishment against such powerhouses as Alberta and the host squad. Goaltender Bob O'Leary and the Holy Cross defenders were outstanding, while the forwards notched timely goals to win several close games. The squad received a tremendous homecoming upon their return, and the following season nearly duplicated the feat. The 1989 Holy Cross team lost a heartbreaker in the finals to Ontario, but proved to the nation that Newfoundland's win the previous year was no fluke.

4. *Newfoundland wins the 1976 Brier*: When the Jack MacDuff rink

finished the 1976 Canadian mens' curling championship with a 9-2 record, it was cause for tremendous satisfaction since that mark was five wins more than Newfoundland's previous best victory total. The fact that impressive record also gave the provincial foursome our first-ever Brier championship touched off celebrations by Newfoundlanders everywhere, particularly in St. John's, and forever changed the status of our curlers at national events from "pushover" to "contender." Membership in curling clubs throughout the province increased dramatically, and the game continues to reap the benefits of having a Newfoundland team winning one of Canada's most prestigious sporting events. Toby MacDonald, Doug Hudson, Ken Templeton and Jack MacDuff remain the only rink from this province to capture the top prize in Canadian curling.

5. *Corner Brook Royals win 1986 Allan Cup*: In 1985 the Corner Brook Royals won the first three games of the Allan Cup final at Humber Gardens in the paper city before losing in seven games. The following season, the club again reached the finals for the top award in Canadian amateur senior hockey, this time in Nelson, British Columbia. The western team proved to be no match for the Royals, who swept the series in four games including a 7-0 whitewash in the finale. Corner Brook had advanced to the Cup championship by defeating the Stephenville Jets to win the Herder Trophy, and then locked horns with a tough Ontario team in a hard-fought seven game showdown in Brantford. Upon returning home, the Royals were given a hero's welcome, including a five-mile long motorcade from Stephenville Airport. With the demise of the senior league, it is doubtful that another team from this province will win the Allan Cup, but the memories of the Royals' championship season will remain for years to come.

6. *Newfoundland wins the Canadian junior men's baseball title in 1966*: St. Pat's Ballpark played host to the Canadian junior championships in 1966 for the first time, and while the field rated highly, many of the visitors didn't feel the same way about the Newfoundland team. Coached by Gordon Breen ("Mr. Baseball"), the province fielded an all-star team primarily comprised of players from the St. John's and Corner Brook leagues. To the surprise of just about everyone, Newfoundland advanced to the championship game against Ontario. A key hit by Ed Hurley of St. John's provided the margin of victory, giving the province its first national title, not just in baseball, but in *any* sport. The fact that the win came at home and was such a major upset made the championship even more sweet.

7. *Professional hockey comes to Newfoundland*: On 30 May 1991, the American Hockey League officially approved the request of the Toronto Maple Leafs to move its AHL affiliate to St. John's from Newmarket, Ontario. Five months later (October 18th), the newly-minted St. John's Maple Leafs played their first game in the city before an overflow crowd at Memorial Stadium. Six seasons later, the fan interest is as strong as ever, and the Leafs continue to provide quality entertainment to Newfoundland hockey fans. In addition to a high calibre of hockey, followers of the "baby Leafs" have watched several alumni become NHL regulars, either with Toronto or other clubs. As a bonus, the team generates a great deal of revenue to area businesses; and donates thousands of dollars annually to various charitable organizations.

8. *Dwayne Norris and Maria Maunder win Olympic silver medals*: At the 1994 Winter Olympics in Lillehammer, Norway, Canada's hockey team lost the gold medal game to Sweden 3-2 in a shootout. Right-winger Dwayne Norris of St. John's made a strong contribution to the team's advancement to the title game not only by his tireless skating and defense, but by some key scoring in a victory over France and a tie against the U.S. Thousands of Newfoundlanders were caught up in the excitement and remained glued to their televisions not only to see Canada do well, but to watch Dwayne Norris in action.

Equally exciting to provincial sports fans was the performance by Logy Bay's Maria Maunder at the finals of the womens' eights rowing competition at the 1996 Summer Olympics in Atlanta. The team put on a tremendous finishing spurt to move from fourth place to second, just failing to overtake Romania for the gold medal. Maria's years of training at university in Ontario and with the national team in B.C. paid off with a strong showing in Atlanta. Having the race televised live allowed Newfoundlanders throughout the province to watch the excitement and to share the emotions of the rowers.

9. *Canada's national soccer team advances to 1986 World Cup*: King George V Field in St. John's played host to the final game of the qualifying round between Canada and Honduras on 14 September 1985. If the Canadian team won, they would be one of the 24 teams entitled to compete at the World Cup in Mexico the following year. If not, they would have to try again in four years. Most of the Canadian players had never been to Newfoundland, and certainly were not familiar with their "home" field. Nearly 8000 fans cheered their every move, and the team responded to edge Honduras 2-1 to qualify for the select tournament. Because of the limited seating

capacity, it is unlikely future games of this type will be played there. However, Canada has not made an appearance in the World Cup since.

10. *Ferd Hayward's performance as the first Newfoundlander on Canada's Olympic team*: Over forty years have passed since the 1952 summer Olympics in Helsinki, Finland, and many Newfoundlanders born since then are not familiar with the athletic accomplishments of racewalker Ferd Hayward of St. John's. He was the first Newfoundlander to compete for Canada in the Olympics, and was proud of the fact that he did not leave the province to train elsewhere. Hayward was the capital city's first athlete of the year in 1951, after having been Newfoundland's premiere racewalking star for nearly 20 years. He won several national and international events during his long career, and in 1988 was one of the first Canadians selected to participate in the Olympic torch relay, en route to the Winter Games in Calgary.

Ten significant female athletes from Newfoundland and Labrador

1. *Joy Morey Burt*: Because of her high level of achievement in two very different sports, Joy Morey of Lark Harbour ranks as one of the best and most versatile female athletes this Province has ever produced. As a soccer player in Corner Brook during the 1970s, Morey was a gifted ball-handler also known for her speed. In fact, the Newfoundland Soccer Association named her as the Province's top female player of the 1970s. After getting married and then taking up powerlifting while attending Memorial University in the 1980s, Joy Burt dominated the sport provincially, became Canadian champion, and reached the pinnacle by winning a world title. Impressive achievements for anyone, especially for somebody raised in a small western Newfoundland community.

2. *Patti Polych*: Throughout the entire decade of the 1970s and continuing into the 1980s, Patti Polych was easily Newfoundland's premiere softball player. Known primarily for her pitching, she began her career in Labrador City in 1970 before switching to the mens' league as a 16-year old. After moving to the capital city prior to the Canada Games in 1977, she proceeded to pitch two perfect games in one season, helped the Province to its highest-ever finish at several Canadian championships, and played on Canada's national team in over a dozen international tournaments during the late 1970s. Although she hasn't lived in Newfoundland since 1983,

many of her accomplishments on the diamond have yet to be matched.

3. *Joanne McDonald*: From 1973 to 1985, Joanne McDonald was not only a consistent medal winner in wheelchair athletics, but did a great deal to educate the public about the capabilities of people with disabilities. A member of the provincial Sports Hall of Fame, she was named Newfoundland's top female athlete of the 1970s for her accomplishments on a provincial, national and international level. The St. Mary's native not only excelled on the track, but worked diligently behind the scenes to raise the profile of disabled athletes within the provincial sports fraternity.

4. *Kathy Noseworthy*: A standout in both volleyball and soccer, this St. John's native received national recognition while still in high school, earning a spot on Canada's junior volleyball team. By 1979, she was a member of the country's senior team and was also selected as the province's top female athlete. She starred with the MUN volleyball team for four years, and later coached the squad. She was equally at home on the soccer field as a mainstay of both the provincial and Memorial University teams, moving from midfield to defence as the situation required.

5. *Violet (Vi) Pike*: This long-time Grand Falls resident has represented Newfoundland an amazing 28 times over her career, and in two different sports. Between 1961 and 1985, she was a member of 18 provincial curling rinks that competed for either the national womens' or national seniors' title. As a golfer, she participated in an additional 10 championships. Not surprisingly, she is a member of both the Newfoundland and Canadian Curling Halls of Fame, as well as the provincial Sports Hall of Fame.

6. *Andrea Hutchens*: As a member of the University of Winnipeg's basketball team for four years (1991-95), Andrea Hutchens of St. John's played a valuable role in helping the club win 88 consecutive games, a record for a Canadian sports team. The Wesmen also were crowned Canadian champions for three of her four years with them, all as a starter. Selected an all-star at the university level, she was the final cut made by the coaching staff of Canada's Olympic basketball team for the 1996 Atlanta Games.

7. *Marg Davis*: An accomplished performer in seven different sports, most notably softball, Marg Davis has earned recognition as one of Newfoundland's finest athletes. In 1978, she became the first Newfoundlander to win a medal in international softball competition, helping Canada to a second place finish at the world championship. A member of the national, provincial, and St. John's Softball Halls

of Fame, she was voted Newfoundland's top player for the first 25 years of provincial competition. In field hockey, she led the Province to a surprise bronze-medal showing at the 1977 Canada Summer Games. Marg Davis also excelled in such diverse sports as soccer, curling, squash, golf and ice hockey. She later coached several provincial teams to berths in national championships.

8. *Gillian Grant*: Another multi-sport athlete, Gillian Grant of St. John's achieved provincial recognition as both a champion racewalker and cross-country skier. She set provincial records in the 3000 and 5000 metres, and twice represented Canada at racewalking events internationally. As a marathon cross-country skier, she won two individual provincial titles, and shared three more in the team competition. Gillian Grant has also won provincial awards in cycling, golf, water polo and triathlon.

9. *Sue Rendell*: This Gander native was a top volleyball player for both Memorial University and Canada's national team. A teammate of Kathy Noseworthy for most of this time, the duo made a strong 1-2 combination that was especially productive at the university level. Often overshadowed by Noseworthy, Sue Rendell was named to the Canadian all-star team for university players in 1982. She later took up coaching.

10. *Margaret Hitchens*: A tennis career spanning 40 years and resulting in 25 Newfoundland Open titles highlights the athletic achievements of Margaret Hitchens of St. John's. Until recent years, provincial tennis has not garnered a great deal of media attention, so Hitchens' accomplishments on the courts have remained unheralded. In addition to many awards at the local level, she has represented the province at national events in three different decades (1960s-80s), and continues to participate in and enjoy the game today.

Ten significant male athletes from Newfoundland and Labrador

1. *George and Alex Faulkner* (hockey): Although Alex was the only member of this Bishop's Falls brother combination to play in the NHL, many hockey observers feel that the only reason George didn't get a chance is because he happened to be a minor league prospect of the talent-rich Montreal Canadiens. At that time (the mid-1950s) the Habs were building a dynasty on their way to a record five straight Stanley Cups, and the chances for rookies to make the big team were remote. Nevertheless, George was successful in any

league in which he played, in or out of Newfoundland. His most notable hockey achievement came late in his career, in 1966, when he led Canada's national team in scoring at the world championships in Yugoslavia. Provincially, he spent ten seasons as playing-coach with the Conception Bay CeeBees, winning four Herder Trophies.

Alex Faulkner's name became well-known across Canada and in Detroit for his scoring prowess with the Red Wings during the 1963 Stanley Cup playoffs when he notched five goals, including three game-winners. Although injuries greatly shortened his NHL career, he spent several productive seasons in the Western Hockey League (WHL). In addition, he played for Herder Trophy-winning teams in both Grand Falls and Conception Bay, earning a total of seven NAHA championships before retiring.

3. *Paul McCloy* (distance running): Durability and consistency have been key factors in the athletic career of Paul McCloy. The holder of numerous Newfoundland records in middle-distance running, and multiple winner of most track events held here, he was also a member of the Canadian team at the 1988 Olympic Games in Seoul, South Korea. Among his major accomplishments are the fastest time in the prestigious "Tely 10" (10 mile) race, as well as his incredible *seven* selections as St. John's top male athlete spanning the period from 1979-91.

4. *Wils Molloy* (soccer): One of the key performers on the St. Lawrence soccer powerhouse of the 1970s, Wils Molloy was a true "impact" player. In addition to helping his Laurentians win nine provincial championships, the Burin Peninsula star attracted national and international attention as a member of Canada's 1972 Olympic soccer team. Perhaps the highlight of his career on the national stage was scoring five goals in a Challenge Cup match against Nova Scotia, despite playing in only the second half.

5. *Doug Grant* (hockey): The only goaltender from this province to ever play in the NHL, Corner Brook's Doug Grant had an outstanding hockey career at the amateur, university and professional levels. He helped the Corner Brook Royals capture two Herder Trophy titles in 1966 and 1968; was an all-star with MUN in 1972; was named the AHL's top rookie in 1973 and the MVP of the Central Hockey League in 1980. He also had stints with both Detroit and St. Louis in the NHL, posting two shutouts.

6. *Ross Crocker* (softball): Equally intimidating to opposing teams whether standing on the mound or at home plate, Ross Crocker's

softball career spanned 26 years. The Heart's Delight native moved to St. John's as a teenager and quickly established himself in the senior league. He holds several league records in both pitching and hitting including most wins, strikeouts, shutouts and total base hits. In national competition, Ross often played shortstop or outfield in games he did not pitch so as to keep his potent bat in the lineup. A talented and versatile player, many of his local and provincial milestones may never be surpassed.

7. *Mel Fitzgerald* (wheelchair sports): The athletic career of Mel Fitzgerald paralleled that of his friend and fellow competitor, Joanne McDonald. Both were faced with not only competing on the track, but in the boardrooms and offices of various sports governing bodies and the corporate community to obtain acceptance and acknowledgement for their efforts. As a racer, Mel Fitzgerald represented both his Province and his Country at many national and international events, earning a variety of medals and awards. His tireless work ethic on and off the track has served as a model to able-bodied and disabled people alike.

8. *Scott Ledrew* (triathlon): Surprisingly, Scott Ledrew of Corner Brook first exhibited his abilities in this endurance sport while competing in Europe long before he achieved recognition in Newfoundland. Upon his return, he proved not only to be among the Province's best athletes, but also an excellent ambassador for the sport, helping to attract more competitors as well as media and corporate attention. The explosive growth of the sport in recent years and its present healthy state provincially owes a great deal to Scott Ledrew.

9. *Gerry Basha* (baseball): A star catcher for many years in both the Corner Brook senior league and in provincial tournaments, Gerry Basha was known for his outstanding defensive abilities as well as his excellent hitting skills. Gifted with a strong throwing arm, Basha was responsible for many would-be base stealers trotting back to the dugout from second base shaking their heads in amazement. One of the key components in the success of the Barons at all-Newfoundland competitions, Gerry Basha ranks as one of the greatest baseball players this Province has ever produced.

10. *Tols Chapman* (multiple sports): Voted Newfoundland's top male athlete of the 1970s, Tols Chapman excelled in a variety of team and individual sports. In an athletic career touching on four decades (1950s-80s), he first gained provincial recognition as an all-star shortstop in baseball and goaltender in hockey. The St. John's native also displayed uncommon skill at tennis, squash and racquetball, earning a variety of local and provincial honours. He coached senior

hockey and guided Newfoundland's ladies' softball team at the 1977 Canada Summer Games. His abilities on the basketball court and the golf course served to enhance his reputation for versatility and outstanding athletic achievements.

Art Rockwood's Lists of "Stuff"

I thought I'd wrap up this volume with some of my own lists, tidbits of trivia and a few anecdotes. A lot of what follows has come up on the Trivia show or "The Rockwood Files" over the years. Just little bits and anecdotes designed to bring a knowing nod, a smile or a chuckle.

The "Rockwood Files" list of little-known historical landmarks and facts

I decided one day to have a contest on my CBC Radio morning show "The Rockwood Files" in which I would ask people to send along information about some little-known event or fact from Newfoundland History. I got a great response from people all over the Island and even from a couple of Labrador communities (surprising, because CBC Labrador doesn't carry the show due to the time difference). Here are some of the responses. The first one I contributed myself to give people an idea of what I was looking for.

1. *Gunner's Rock, Heart's Content.* In the latter part of the nineteenth and early part of the twentieth century, mail which was destined for communities on the south side of Trinity Bay was couriered to Heart's Content from Carbonear. From there it was taken and distributed down the shore to places like Hants Harbour, Winterton and New Melbourne.
The towering hills behind Heart's Content are known as The Mizzen. From the top you can get a beautiful view of the community and its harbour, and it was to this hill that the Carbonear mailman would arrive by horse and cart to bring the mail to his Heart's Content counterpart. When he arrived, the Carbonear man would stand on a large rock and fire a gun to announce his arrival to the people

below. Then he would sit down on the rock, stoke up his pipe and wait for the arrival of the Heart's Content mailman.

It's been said that, having little else to do, many of these Carbonear men would carve their initials in the rock, and that as late as the thirties and early forties they could still be seen. Unfortunately, in more recent years no one has been able to find the rock.

The carving of the initials may be apocryphal, but the existence of the Gunner's Rock itself is certain. My father, now in his 70s, would often go there as a young boy with his buddies.

Most residents of Heart's Content today don't even know about the rock. The one person who knew most about the rock and had been there many times was Ed Underhay. He knew exactly where it was and said he had seen the carved initials. Unfortunately Mr. Underhay passed away before he could show any of the younger residents where Gunner's Rock was located.

2. *The Newfoundland Map in the Hibb's Cove Rock* (submitted by Nellie Strowbridge of Pasadena). This sculpture was carved by nature into the face of a rock which sits near a narrow lane in Hibb's Cove. The relief is an almost perfect map of the Island of Newfoundland. (Nellie included a photograph of the relief taken from *Newfoundland TV Topics* 15 Jan 1980, but unfortunately the photo had faded too much to be reproduced here.)

3. *The South River "Widow's" Chair* (submitted by Richard Carroll of Gander). In South River, Conception Bay, there's a large shed, and atop that shed is a chair. It has been said that on stormy nights a woman can be seen sitting in the chair gazing out to sea. Legend had it that the woman's husband had gone off to sea and had never returned and that she went there night after night to wait for him.

The real story is that at one time the shed had been used as a furniture factory. The owner thought it might be an idea to advertise his product by putting a chair on the roof.

4. *The Plan to turn Labrador into a Penal Colony* (submitted by Father Peter Golden of Trepassey). Francois Lapailleur was a Canadian who was captured and sentenced, along with 78 other Canadians, to be deported to a prison colony in Australia. Their crime was having taken part in the Upper Canada uprisings of 1838 and 1839. During his two-year incarceration, LaPailleur kept a diary in which he documented life at the Longbottom prison stockade. One of the facts LaPailleur notes in his record is that in 1841 the British Parliament debated making Labrador a Penal Colony to ease the burden on Australia. The plan was never carried out.

5. *The St. Shott's Anchor* (submitted by Verna (Molloy) Hayward). A

huge anchor stands on a concrete platform in the schoolyard at St. Shotts. Many people have wondered about the origin of the anchor. Tradition has it that after a shipwreck near the community the anchor went to the bottom. After years of being battered by heavy waves and rough seas the anchor eventually came to rest in a cove near a large rock which came to be known as Big Anchor Rock. Some years later the anchor was needed to aid in pulling bales of cotton from another shipwreck. Several men and horses dragged it to the required location and it remained there until the council decided it would make a great tourist attraction. They painted it black and moved it to its present site.

6. *The Bay du Nord Indian Cross* (submitted by Mrs. John Quann). At Bay du Nord in Fortune Bay there's a large cross made of stones. Known as the Indian Cross, it is at the top of a plateau accessible only by climbing a steep ravine. The stones weigh anywhere from ten to twenty pounds and must have been carried there over some distance, because there are no others in the area. On 26 July each year the Micmac make a pilgrimage to the shrine, which is said to have healing powers.

Three great moments in Newfoundland radio and television history

Very much a personal list—of moments which I have heard or seen and which, to my mind at least, are classics.

1. *Turner and the cat.* Jim Turner was a newsman at CJON in the 1970s. People will remember Jim's casual delivery and the dark glasses which he always wore. One night he was delivering the late-night news on television when a cat jumped up on his desk and proceeded to purr, meow, and stick her rear end in Jim's face. The unflappable Turner said hello to the pussycat and continued on with the newscast with a wry smile on his face. At one point the cat jumped down from the desk and went away. But in a few minutes she popped back up again. Jim never blinked, just went on as though nothing out of the ordinary was happening and completed the newscast in fine style. Unfortunately this was before VCRs, so no record of it exists aside from memory. By the way, I am told the reason the cat was there was that management had a few brought in to keep the mice out of the CJON Building on Buckmaster's Circle.

2. *Don Jamieson and "Danny Boy."* In his non-political life as a television newscaster and personality at CJON, Don Jamieson was known for his wonderful television specials. St. Patrick's Day or

Christmas or whatever the occasion he'd bring out the family and some special guests to appear for an entertaining half hour or so. During the show, Jamieson himself might even do a recitation or two. One night I watched him as he recited "Danny Boy." He was seated in a comfortable chair and, at one of the piece's high points, he decided to stand up to deliver the remainder of the poem. The boom mike operator must have been asleep, because as Jamieson stood up his head smacked into the dangling mike. Don never missed a word... his voice only jerked a little as head and microphone met with a loud "whomp!" In the manner of the true professional that he was, he just went on as though nothing had happened.

3. *Pat Murphy's afternoon show, CJON Summer 1971.* I can count on my two hands the number of truly outstanding radio shows I have heard over the years and, being the radio junkie that I am, I've heard thousands of hours. One sunny summer afternoon in 1971 I was sitting in my car outside a doctor's office on Lemarchant Road, the radio was tuned to CJON, Pat Murphy was on and the show he did that day was brilliant. The music, the comedy, his crazy voices, even the commercials. Everything fit perfectly. Definitely a classic piece of radio which would have stood up in any radio market. Unfortunately a memory is all I have. I did not have a cassette recorder handy to tape it for my collection.

Great Newfoundland web sites

I have been surfing the internet since 1988. Its only been eight years, but what a difference there is in the net of today and the net of '88! Back in the "old days" we found things using Archie and Veronica to search FTP and Gopher sites. And there were no graphics—everything was text-based. Nowadays, with high speed modems and graphical browsers, millions of people are finding treasure on the internet.

Among those treasures are hundreds of thousands of 'home pages' or 'sites.' These pages can offer everything from pictures and biographical or informational material, to live radio and television broadcasts. Here are ten of my favourite Newfoundland Labrador sites.

1. (http://www.det.mun.ca/staff/triche/NFlinks.htm) *Tina Riche's Page of Newfoundland Links.* Tina has assembled what is, by far, the best page of Newfoundland links. This is the quickest way to find your way to almost every Newfoundland and Labrador related site.

2. (http://www.ucs.mun.ca/~hrollman/) *Han Rollmann's Religious Studies Page*. Dr. Hans Rollmann is with MUN's Religious Studies department. His international award-winning site started modestly and has grown into a treasure trove for Newfoundland history buffs. While a lot relates to our religious heritage, it includes some of the earliest writings done in Newfoundland. And visually it's a delight.
3. (http://www.newcomm.net/eastcost/ect.htm)*The East Coast Trail Association Page*. Another international award winner, which includes historical information on the Avalon Peninsula, general information about trails and hiking and some stunning photographs.
4. (http://www.iosphere.net/~jholwell/links/nllinks.html) *Newfoundlanders Adrift...Ties to the Home"*. Probably the most comprehensive site for Newfoundlandia. Originally from Corner Brook, John Holwell is now living in Nepean, Ontario (which he refers to as Ottawa's Mount Pearl). Like most successful personal home pages, this one started out small scale but it's grown into 600 files of information, including some wonderful pages of historical information.
5. (http://www.wordplay.com/) *Wordplay*. Yet another visually appealing page with lots to offer. Wordplay is a Duckworth Street bookstore, and was the first Newfoundland commercial venture I found on the net. In addition to information about what books the store has on offer, you'll find information about the arts scene generally, tourism and business. You can "visit" the James Baird Art Gallery.
6. (http://www.databits.com/yaffles3.html) *Yaffles & Yaffles Page*. This is the Databits E-Zine (electronically-distributed magazine). Go to this site and you can link to Margaret Ayad's Newfoundland Recipes Page, information about the Irish Princess (Sheila NaGira), 'Mayo' Lind's letters from the first World War, and several other things of interest to Newfoundlanders.
7. (http://www.ozfm.newcomm.net/) *OZ-FM*. They may not have been the first Newfoundland radio station to have a presence on the net, but they've certainly been a commanding presence. OZ offers their programming live and in stereo for anyone who has a RealAudio player on their computer. And if you don't have it they'll show you where you can get it.
8. (http://www.cabot.nf.ca/~davidM/) *David Molloy's Historic Lighthouses Page*. Interesting history and a travelogue of Newfoundland and Labrador through a tour of the lighthouses around the Province. Nice graphics and lots of text.
9. (http://www.mediatouch.com/avalon/) *The Colony of Avalon Page*. An entertaining, as well as informative, site offering details about the historic community of Ferryland.

10. (http://www.solutions.net/rec-travel/northamerica/canada/new-foundland/newfoundland.html) *The rec-travel library page of tourist information* Rec.travel is an internet newsgroup devoted to finding and disseminating tourism information from around the world, including a page especially for Newfoundland and Labrador. As of this writing, some of it is out of date but, nonetheless, it has lots of information about where to go, what to do, and what to see based upon people's experience rather than tourist brochures.

Although it would be unfair to list these, I would like to mention my own homepage **(http://www.ucs.mun.ca/~rockwood)**. Also two new websites run by my publisher, *Harry Cuff Publications Limited* **(http://www.cuff.com)** and **(http://www.zyqote.com)** offer items of interest to the local and global Internet community.

Two of my most embarrassing moments

We all have a few little embarrassments over the years, but when you are on-air radio personality and budding writer your opportunties to be revealed to the world as a first-rate ass are doozies. Here are the two real standouts for me. I share them now with head bowed in deep humility.

1. *The only day I swore on the air.* At CBG in Gander I hosted the morning show for seven years. I was usually helped by a newsreader, and for sports, Bruce MacDonald in Grand Falls. At exactly 7:45 Bruce would simulcast his sports on CBG and on CBT in Grand Falls. We had to flip the switch to him at 7:45 on the button. One morning Dave Lawton was reading the news for me and his last story went long. As soon as he finished I cut his mike, turned on my own, quickly said "7:45. Here's Bruce MacDonald with sports," hit the switch for Grand Falls (forgetting to turn off my own mike switch) and got Bruce in the first line of his opening story, the sweat beading on my brow.

   In my frustration my one-word utterance, with all the gusto I could muster, was "Jesus!!!!!" I can still hear the echo as it reverberated in my headset. I could feel myself blanch. I was in trouble. You do not swear on the CBC in a family-oriented morning show—and we were the most listened to morning show in the area. I finished the program and when the manager arrived I told him of my indisgression. He asked if there had been any complaints. I said there hadn't. He said "Well, let's see what happens. If anyone complains we may have to do something." I figured I'd probably get away with a week's suspension. Not a single call complaining. The only comment I heard about it came from co-worker Gerry Smith next morning. He said he'd been at the Legion club the previous afternoon and was approached by a listener. The listener said "Listen, Ger. Will you tell Rockwood that the correct pronounciation of the name in sports is Hayzoos, not Jesus."

2. *Killing John Ford before his time.* Ever since I started my trivia collecting I've been gathering bits and pieces of information on this thing and that, clipping it from newspapers, magazines and so on, then putting it into files—dozens and dozens of files. The problem is in trying to keep it all in order. In August of 1993 I was working on my second book. On the desk in my room I had scattered several references: books, magazines and file folders. One of the topics in my book was to be about John Ford, a remarkable Newfoundlander in that he survived the atomic bomb at Nagasaki. Somewhere in all the information I had gathered I had found an obituary of a John Ford who had served with the forces in Asia. He had just passed away. As a footnote to the piece on Mr. Ford in my book I included the line "He died in 1993." I hadn't bothered to call his family for verification... I didn't want to disturb them in their time of grief. And in the rush to get the book completed and in the hands of the publisher by the middle of September I forgot to follow it up.

As soon as the book was released I received a call from Bill Learning. He informed me that not only was John Ford still alive and well, but that he and Mr. Ford had laid a wreath at the war memorial on Remembrance Day. I felt as embarrassed as I had ever felt in my life. To think that John Ford survived an atomic blast, only to be "done in" by Art Rockwood! I called John Ford to apologize. He mentioned that several people had inquired as to his state of health after the book came out. He was somewhat amused and told me not to worry about it. We had a grand chat and not once did he admonish me for being so stunned.

A chuckle to end with...

A Bell Island caller to the Trivia show one afternoon asked the following question: "What Newfoundlander's name is mentioned in songs more than any other?" He prefaced the question by saying he hoped co-host Mike Power and I had a sense of humour. We were stumped. Mike suggested maybe "Sonny." Nope. The caller said we should think of western songs done by people like Roy Rogers, Tex Ritter and Wilf Carter. We were still stumped. The caller let us off the hook by giving us the answer. A Bell Islander by the name of Leo Lahey. Well, I've heard thousands of songs in my life, but I said I couldn't remember ever hearing one that mentions the name Leo Lahey. Our caller said "Sure you have. Whenever you hear a yodeller, what does he sing? (You have to yodel this) "Leo Lahey whooooo." Mike and I cracked up. The very next caller, another regular with as wild a sense of humour, picked up on the joke by saying "I thought the line was (yodel again) 'The Little Old Lady Leo Lahey knew'."

And on that note we end the Book of Newfoundland and Labrador Lists. When I completed my first two trivia books, people would always ask "Will there be a sequel?" I expect the same question this time, too. Without question the possibilities are endless and being the list-maker that I am I've already made a few pages of notes. One area I would like to develop more (if there is a sequel) is the area of personal lists. Lists of people's favourites in music, books, television, movies, actors, politicians, etc. etc. You get the idea. See what I mean? The mind reels with possibilities. If you have any comments, be they compliment or criticism, or even if you have suggestions for some lists you'd like to see, just drop me a line. You can contact me through the publisher—who offers one last little list of his own.

Famous last words

Sir Humphrey Gilbert (1583): "We are as near to heaven by sea as by land."

Captain Arthur Jackman (1907) to his nephew, Father William Jackman, who had just administered last rites: "Put the flags on 'er, Billy boy, and let 'er go."